The Oklahoma City Bombing

by Richard Brownell

LUCENT BOOKS

An imprint of Thomson Gale, a part of The Thomson Corporation

THOMSON

GALE

Detroit • New York • San Francisco • New Haven, Conn. • Waterville, Maine • London

© 2007 Thomson Gale, a part of The Thomson Corporation.

Thomson and Star Logo are trademarks and Gale and Lucent Books are registered trademarks used herein under license.

For more information, contact
Lucent Books
27500 Drake Rd.
Farmington Hills, MI 48331-3535
Or you can visit our Internet site at http://www.gale.com

LIBRARY OF CONGRESS CATALOGING-IN-PUBLICATION DATA

Brownell, Richard.
  The Oklahoma City bombing / by Richard Brownell.
    p. cm. — (Crime scene investigations)
  Includes bibliographical references and index.
  ISBN 978-1-59018-843-9 (hardcover)
  1. Oklahoma City Federal Building Bombing, Oklahoma City, Okla.,1995—Juvenile literature. 2. Bombings—Oklahoma—Oklahoma City—Juvenile literature. 3. Bombing investigation—Oklahoma—Oklahoma City—Juvenile literature. I. Title.
  HV6432.6.B76 2007
  976.6'38053—dc22

2007006814

ISBN-10: 1-59018-843-8
Printed in the United States of America

Contents

Foreword

The popularity of crime scene and investigative crime shows on television has come as a surprise to many who work in the field. The main surprise is the concept that crime scene analysts are the true crime solvers, when in truth, it takes dozens of people, doing many different jobs, to solve a crime. Often, the crime scene analyst's contribution is a small one. One Minnesota forensic scientist says that the public "has gotten the wrong idea. Because I work in a lab similar to the ones on *CSI*, people seem to think I'm solving crimes left and right— just me and my microscope. They don't believe me when I tell them that it's the investigators that are solving crimes, not me."

Crime scene analysts do have an important role to play, however. Science has rapidly added a whole new dimension to gathering and assessing evidence. Modern crime labs can match a hair of a murder suspect to one found on a murder victim, for example, or recover a latent fingerprint from a threatening letter, or use a powerful microscope to match tool marks made during the wiring of an explosive device to a tool in a suspect's possession.

Probably the most exciting of the forensic scientist's tools is DNA analysis. DNA can be found in just one drop of blood, a dribble of saliva on a toothbrush, or even the residue from a fingerprint. Some DNA analysis techniques enable scientists to tell with certainty, for example, whether a drop of blood on a suspect's shirt is that of a murder victim.

While these exciting techniques are now an essential part of many investigations, they cannot solve crimes alone. "DNA doesn't come with a name and address on it," says the Minnesota forensic scientist. "It's great if you have someone in custody to match the sample to, but otherwise, it doesn't help. That's the investigator's job. We can have all the great DNA evidence in the world, and without a suspect, it will just sit on the shelf. We've all seen cases with very little forensic evidence get solved by the resourcefulness of a detective."

While forensic specialists get the most media attention today, the work of detectives still forms the core of most criminal investigations. Their job, in many ways, has changed little over the years. Most cases are still solved through the persistence and determination of a criminal detective whose work may be anything but glamorous. Many cases require routine, even mind-numbing tasks. After the July 2005 bombings in London, for example, police officers sat in front of video players watching thousands of hours of closed-circuit television tape from security cameras throughout the city, and as a result were able to get the first images of the bombers.

The Lucent Books Crime Scene Investigations series explores the variety of ways crimes are solved. Titles cover particular crimes such as murder, specific cases such as the killing of three civil rights workers in Mississippi, or the role specialists such as medical examiners play in solving crimes. Each title in the series demonstrates the ways a crime may be solved, from the various applications of forensic science and technology to the reasoning of investigators. Sidebars examine both the limits and possibilities of the new technologies and present crime statistics, career information, and step-by-step explanations of scientific and legal processes.

The Crime Scene Investigations series strives to be both informative and realistic about how members of law enforcement—criminal investigators, forensic scientists, and others—solve crimes, for it is essential that student researchers understand that crime solving is rarely quick or easy. Many factors—from a detective's dogged pursuit of one tenuous lead to a suspect's careless mistakes to sheer luck to complex calculations computed in the lab—are all part of crime solving today.

The Seeds of Hatred

America has a history of dissent among its citizens that stretches back to its founding. At various times groups that found themselves alienated by the direction the country was taking politically or socially have acted to preserve an ideal or social convention dear to them. In the country's democratic tradition these actions have taken many forms—peaceful protests, boycotts, and the support of sympathetic candidates for public office.

There have been times, however, when dissent has taken violent forms such as kidnapping, murder, and bombings. These tactics were employed by a fringe element of extremists who believed the federal government was systematically stripping away constitutional rights in order to solidify its power over the people. The creation in recent years of powerful new federal law enforcement agencies like the Drug Enforcement Administration (DEA) and the Bureau of Alcohol, Tobacco, Firearms, and Explosives (ATF), as well as the institution of tougher gun ownership laws and higher and broader federal taxes, were given as examples of the government's tightening grip over its citizens. One man who subscribed to this extremist mindset was Randy Weaver.

Ruby Ridge

Weaver was a follower of the white supremacist ideology and was known to have attended meetings of the Aryan Nations near Coeur d'Alene, Idaho. Among the acquaintances he made there was a man looking for Weaver's help in obtaining illegal firearms. Weaver was having serious financial difficulties and agreed to help him. The man was actually an informant for the ATF, and after the deal was made Weaver was arrested on weapons charges. His court date was set for February 19, 1991, but the U.S. attorney's office notified Weaver, in error, that he was to appear March 20. When the actual court date passed and he did not appear, Weaver was categorized as a fugitive. Believing there was a conspiracy against him, Weaver took his wife and their three children to a cabin in the mountain region of Ruby Ridge, Idaho, where they remained over the next year and a half.

During that time the U.S. marshals put the area under surveillance and devised a plan to capture Weaver. Writer David Lohr, in his article for the Court TV Crime Library, "Randy Weaver: Siege at Ruby Ridge," gives a summary of the assessment of the marshals' investigation. "The team concluded that

Randy Weaver, a follower of the white supremacist ideology, testifies in court.

the Weavers had been looking for a war with law enforcement and that Randy had most likely established numerous fortifications and defensive positions on his property. It is also concluded that since Randy was a former Green Beret, he had probably placed booby traps or command-detonated explosive devices throughout the property."[1]

This assessment caused high anxiety among the marshals, who believed a confrontation was imminent. Unfortunately, Weaver's own paranoia led to the same conclusion. On August 21, 1991, a gunfight erupted between the marshals and members of Weaver's family, leading to an eleven-day siege during which Weaver's wife and fourteen-year-old son and a U.S. marshal were killed. The event gathered national media attention and fueled widespread resentment of the federal government.

The Siege at Waco

By the time Weaver was in custody and his case went to trial in the spring of 1993, a similar episode was unfolding near Waco, Texas. The Branch Davidians, a religious group of about a hundred men, women, and children who believed that the apocalypse was at hand, had become the focus of a federal investigation into illegal weapons trafficking and the possible abuse of children within the sect. On February 28 ATF agents attempted to storm their compound to execute a search and arrest the group's leader, David Koresh, on weapons charges. A shootout erupted and four agents and several Davidians were killed. The event quickly became the focus of national attention as hundreds of ATF and FBI agents laid siege on the Davidian compound with tanks, armored personnel carriers, and assault choppers.

During the ensuing fifty-one days, negotiators tried unsuccessfully to get Koresh to give himself up. A total of twenty-one children and fourteen adults left the compound, but another seventy-five remained, apparently of their own free will. Electricity and water to the main building were cut off, vehicles were towed away, and the outer shacks were bulldozed.

David Koresh at the Branch Davidian compound in Waco, Texas.

Bright lights shone on the building at night and loudspeakers broadcast hours of loud music and irritating noises meant to psychologically wear down those who were still inside.

Antigovernment activists around the country saw the Waco siege as a glaring example of the federal government's abuse of authority, and hundreds flocked to the site to protest the actions of law enforcement. Timothy McVeigh, a Gulf War veteran who had traveled to Waco to assess the situation for himself, gave voice to their sentiments in an interview with student journalist Michelle Rauch. "It seems the ATF just wants a chance to play with their toys, paid for by government money," McVeigh said. "The government is continually growing bigger and more powerful, and the people need to prepare to defend themselves against government control."[2]

The fact that Koresh had actually engaged in the illegal trafficking of firearms was lost on McVeigh and the other antigovernment protestors. However, law enforcement's heavy-handed tactics also played into Koresh's belief that the end of the world was approaching, and any chance for the standoff to end peacefully rapidly eroded. On April 19, 1993, believing there was no other solution, FBI agents began inserting CS gas (a form of tear gas) into the compound in an attempt to get the Davidians to surrender. Shortly thereafter, the building erupted into flames, and Koresh and seventy-four other Davidians were killed. It was later determined that Koresh and several others actually died of gunshot wounds, some self-inflicted, rather than from the fire.

There was speculation that the fire that killed the Davidians was actually caused by the CS gas, which is a nonlethal irritant that creates a burning sensation in the eyes, nose, and throat. The FBI maintained that the material used was not flammable, despite scientific proof that CS gas can become combustible in confined spaces. In an October 1993 Department of Justice report, the government stated, "[The] fire on April 19, 1993 was deliberately set by persons inside the compound and was not started by the FBI's tear gas insertion operation."[3]

This did not satisfy those like McVeigh, who believed the government callously chose to use maximum force to bring an end to the siege at Waco just as federal authorities had done at Ruby Ridge. These two events became a rallying cry for antigovernment activists, and radical elements called for revenge.

CHAPTER 1

Declaring War on America

In the early 1990s there was a growing concern over the prominence of radical antigovernment separatists in the United States. These separatists preached an ideology of hate, stockpiled weapons, and advocated overthrowing the government in order to protect their own rights. Concerned individuals and members of the law enforcement community believed the deadly standoffs at Ruby Ridge, Idaho, and the Branch Davidian compound outside Waco, Texas, were prime examples of the danger posed by these extremists.

The federal government, however, did not believe that such radicals were a threat to national security. They reasoned that Ruby Ridge and Waco were isolated incidents that were the result of actions by right-wing extremists and poor crisis management by law enforcement agents. Consequently there was no reason for the federal government to think that American citizens could perpetrate a major coordinated attack on the country's institutions, and it did not act to enhance the security of America's civilian infrastructure and federal facilities.

The bombing of New York City's World Trade Center on February 26, 1993, proved that America was not safe from large-scale terrorist attacks. Islamic radicals detonated a truck bomb in the underground parking garage of Tower One of the complex with the intent of weakening the building's structure enough to topple it into Tower Two and destroy both skyscrapers. In that regard, the bombing was a failure, but six people were killed and over one thousand were injured.

The federal government successfully prosecuted the case, but remained lax in developing tighter security to prevent further such attacks. New York senator Charles Schumer noted

The Alfred P. Murrah federal building in Oklahoma City, pictured in 1993.

in 2002 that a "group of dastardly people tried to blow up the World Trade Center, six Americans died, and what did we do as a society? Absolutely nothing. We shrugged our shoulders, we washed our hand with it, and we went on our merry way."[4] Security at the numerous federal facilities around the country remained geared toward low-level incursions such as break-ins or robberies. For instance, at the Alfred P. Murrah federal building in Oklahoma City, Oklahoma, in which offices of over a dozen federal agencies employed close to five hundred people, there was only one daytime security guard on duty.

The Target

Mark S. Hamm, professor of criminology at Indiana State University and author of *Apocalypse in Oklahoma: Waco and Ruby Ridge Revenged*, speculates that had there been more than one security guard on duty at the Murrah federal building on Wednesday, April 19, 1995, it is possible that the odd movements of a large Ryder rental truck might have been noticed.

"Perhaps the most pertinent thing a guard could have noticed was the vehicle's overloaded midsection."[5] Noticeably weighted down and moving slowly across the intersection of Northwest 5th Street and Harvey Avenue, the truck came to a stop at the front of the building at exactly 9:00 A.M. This area was clearly designated as a dropping-off point for vehicles which generally would deliver a passenger and then leave. Large vehicles, like this Ryder truck, would always make deliveries at another part of the building.

Daina Bradley had noticed the truck, but it was of only cursory interest to her at the time. She had come to the Social Security office on the ground floor with her mother, sister, and two children to obtain a Social Security card for her four-month-old son Gabreon. Bradley was only one of the many

This surveillance camera photo shows the Ryder truck driving past an Oklahoma City apartment complex just minutes before the bombing.

04-19-95 WED
08:57:05   24

thousands of Oklahoma residents who took advantage of the services offered by the Murrah building's numerous federal agencies.

The Social Security office, which employed 65 people, shared the first floor with the General Services Administration, which employed 43 people. On the third floor 86 employees worked in offices as wide-ranging as the Government Accounting Office, Health and Human Services, army recruiting, the Defense Department, and the Federal Credit Union. There were an additional 98 employees in the army recruiting office on the fourth floor, along with 28 workers in the Department of Transportation. An additional 81 employees staffed offices on the fifth floor, working at the Department of Agriculture, Housing and Urban Development, U.S. Customs, and the Veterans Office. And on floors six through nine, 231 employees worked for the Drug Enforcement Administration, the Bureau of Alcohol, Tobacco, Firearms, and Explosives, and the U.S. Marine Corps.

The Murrah building was also home to America's Kids day care center, which was located on the second floor. Parents with jobs in the building offices or in the vicinity often brought their children there before going to work. The center overlooked Northwest 5th Street, where the Ryder rental truck was parked and abandoned at 9:01 A.M.

The Blast

Investigators know the exact moment the bomb inside the Ryder truck detonated—9:02:13 A.M.— because the shock of the explosion registered at the Oklahoma Geological Survey Station in the town of Norman, sixteen miles (25.7km) away. The blast virtually vaporized the truck, sending a shock wave, or detonation front, of superhot gas outward and upward at the speed of 9,000 feet (2,743.2m) per second or 7,000 miles (11,265.1km) per hour. The pressure at the source of the explosion was more than 1 million pounds (453,600kg) per square inch (6.45 sq. cm), forcing heat and gas to travel at an incred-

ible rate. At this point, according to Hamm, "the explosion simultaneously pushed the first two floors upward and destroyed three of the four columns supporting the second-floor beam. The steel beam toppled, sending the building into progressive collapse as ceilings crashed into floors."[6] With the main load-bearing beam severed and several of the vertical pillars that stretched from the third floor to the top of the building destroyed, there was nothing to keep the north side of the building from collapsing.

Richard Slay, an employee of the Department of Health and Human Services was at the elevator in the lobby when the bomb went off. "The blast of air came first, and then the explosion," Slay later recalled. "And the building just started sliding into the street."[7]

During the first few seconds after the explosion, 102 people were killed between the third and ninth floors, crushed under the weight of falling debris, cut by glass, metal, and concrete traveling through the air at high speed, or burned by the

On April 19, 1995, a truck bomb exploded in front of the Alfred P. Murrah federal building, killing 168 people.

intense heat and pressure of the fireball itself. Some workers were trapped on what remained of the upper floors as others cascaded down into the crater below.

Florence Rogers, an official with the Federal Credit Union on the third floor, was meeting with eight other employees at the time of the explosion. "I was thrown against the floor in a kind of tornadolike rush. And when I was able to stand up, all the girls that were in my office with me had totally disappeared with the six floors from above us on top of them."[8]

The day care center on the second floor took the full force of the explosion, killing fifteen children and three teachers instantly. An additional eighteen workers died on the first floor, and twenty-four bystanders were also caught in the blast. Nearby automobiles exploded after their gas tanks ignited, and there was extensive damage and multiple injuries in the area surrounding the Murrah building.

Rescue workers sift through the rubble of the destroyed Murrah federal building.

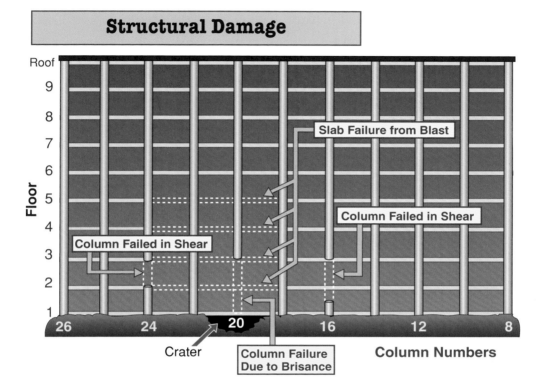

Structural Damage

Slab Failure from Blast

Column Failed in Shear

Column Failed in Shear

Column Failure Due to Brisance

Crater

Column Numbers

Floor

Roof 9 8 7 6 5 4 3 2 1

26 24 20 16 12 8

One hundred windows in the federal courthouse one block south of the Murrah building shattered, and courtrooms and offices were littered with broken glass, plaster, and ceiling tiles. To the north, the roof of the Journal Record building was blown off, and the front of the Athenian building caved in, killing a woman. Hundreds of windows in the Water Resources building were shattered, killing two people in a shower of broken glass. The shock wave was strong enough to lift a 240-pound man (108.86kg) from his bed in one of the rooms at the YMCA and thrust him through the window.

All of this happened within the first few seconds following the explosion. Parts of the Murrah building would continue to cascade downward for several minutes as the smoke from the explosion rose high into the Oklahoma air. James Hargrove, a worker with Health and Human Services, recalls the eerie moments immediately following the explosion. "It was like I was the only person alive. There was no screaming, no moaning, no hissing from gas lines. . . . It was almost silent."[9]

Rescuing the Living and Recovering the Dead

That silence was short-lived, if it ever existed at all. Car and building security alarms had been jarred into action for several blocks in all directions. Sirens from rapidly approaching police, fire, and rescue vehicles closed in on the building. And the moans and screams of trapped victims began to rise from the rubble.

Fireman Steve Bowers was one of the first rescue workers to arrive on the scene. Bowers was a former U.S. Navy combat medic who was on-site when a suicide bomber drove an explosives-laden truck into the U.S. Marine barracks in Beirut, Lebanon, on October 23, 1983, killing 241 American service personnel, most of them in their sleep. "I was trained to deal with this overseas, but not in the heart of America," Bowers said later. "This is Oklahoma City, not a war zone. Not here. No way!"[10]

Bowers and the other first responders came upon a scene that had unfolded into chaos. Survivors of the attack wandered out of the ruins, many in shock and badly injured. A thick haze of smoke and debris filled the air, obscuring what remained of the shattered building. Women rushed toward the building screaming for their children who had been left at the day care center just moments before. People spilled onto the street from nearby buildings, lacerated by broken glass and flying debris. Others came onto the scene trying to figure out just what had happened.

The list of responders from several jurisdictions that arrived in the early minutes and hours is detailed in a report by the Chemical and Biological Arms Control Institute, *Critical Information Flows in the Alfred P. Murrah Building Bombing:*

Alfred P. Murrah and the Building Named in His Honor

The man who would become the namesake of the federal building in downtown Oklahoma City was a distinguished judge who served on the federal bench for thirty-four years. Orphaned at a young age, Murrah worked his way through school and graduated from the University of Oklahoma with honors. He was first appointed to the U.S. district court in 1936 by President Franklin D. Roosevelt, making him the youngest federal judge in American history. He was elevated to the Tenth Circuit Court of Appeals in 1940 and later became its chief judge, serving in that capacity until 1970.

In 1972 $13 million were appropriated for the construction of a federal office building to be named in Murrah's honor. It was completed in 1977, two years after his death, at a cost of $14.5 million and was considered a model of energy efficiency for its time. Almost the entire north, east, and west sides of the building were encased in glass to take advantage of the natural light for heating purposes. It was this feature that made the building an attractive target to Timothy McVeigh, because it could be easily destroyed in an explosion, and the flying glass would create a higher degree of casualties.

In addition to the Oklahoma City fire department, the Oklahoma City police department, and the Federal Bureau of Investigation, the Emergency Medical Services Authority, the Oklahoma State Bureau of Investigation, the Department of Civil Emergency Management, the Oklahoma State highway patrol, the Oklahoma National Guard, and Tinker Air Force Base assisted in various aspects of the response effort on-scene, from the removal of victims to the criminal investigation.[11]

A view of the tremendous damage caused to the Murrah federal building.

There were two major challenges that had to be surmounted in these first vital moments after the bombing. The first was effectively coordinating the rescue personnel from the numerous jurisdictions with a minimum of communications equipment and no viable command structure. The second was assessing the danger that still remained of further collapse of the building as rescue workers bravely charged in to find survivors.

Chunks of concrete continued to tumble from the weakened structure, one of which struck rescue worker Rebecca Anderson, who died of her injuries four days later. Live electrical wires dangled precariously, threatening to electrocute anyone close by. Water poured freely from broken pipes, increasing the electrical hazard and making the broken floors treacherously slick. Noxious fumes from burning plastic, insulation, and other building materials and various chemicals flowed through the air, creating pockets where breathing was difficult.

It was in this atmosphere that Bradley was discovered pinned beneath a pile of rubble. The location where she was discovered was directly beneath a cement slab that was hanging by two 2-inch pieces (5.08cm) of steel reinforcement bars, hardly enough to keep the concrete secure for very long. Several attempts to cut through the steel under which Bradley was pinned were unsuccessful, and the grim decision was made by orthopedic surgeon Andrew Sullivan to amputate her leg in order to set her free.

At the moment Bradley reluctantly conceded to the operation, a bomb scare forced rescue workers to evacuate the building and abandon survivors that needed to be freed. It was not known where the call came from, but after forty-five agonizing minutes, it was determined to be a false alarm and the rescuers returned to their work.

Sullivan realized that due to Bradley's injuries, he could not give her an anesthetic on-site for fear that she would go into shock and die. The operation commenced with Bradley wide awake and screaming in agony while Sullivan amputated her leg. She was pulled from the building to safety and learned later that her mother and both her children had perished in the bombing.

Throughout the day and into the night, when rains came and made the recovery of victims even more difficult, rescuers came across many more such scenes of agony and horror. The

By the Numbers

Oklahoma City Bombing Casualty Report

168
Total number of people killed

19
Children killed

1
Rescue worker killed

98
Federal government employees killed

3
State government employees killed

Source: Oklahoma City National Memorial. www.oklahomacity nationalmemorial.org/hist.htm.

Baylee Almon (above), shown in a family photo, became a symbol of the horrific Oklahoma City bombing.

Photographer Charles H. Porter IV (right) took the moving photo of firefighter Chris Fields holding the lifeless body of Baylee Almon as he brought her out of the rubble of the Murrah building.

hardest moments came during the recovery of the remains of children in the day care center. The captured image of firefighter Chris Fields carrying the body of one-year-old Baylee Almon became the universal symbol for the tragedy that unfolded on April 19, 1995.

The Investigation Begins

As rescue and recovery efforts got underway, state and federal investigators began poring through the wreckage and gathering evidence to solve the crime. As with all criminal investigations, the early hours are crucial in obtaining information while the crime scene is still fresh. Initially the investigation was hampered because rescue workers had brought in large equipment such as earthmovers and cranes to sift through the rubble for survivors, disturbing the crime scene. While the search for survivors was of major importance, the sonar tracking equipment, the thermal sensors, the hydraulic lifts, and the bulldozers all played a role in tainting the scene and obstructing the unfolding investigation.

The FBI took charge early and set up a four-hundred-telephone command center to coordinate the work of explosives experts and scientific teams that would analyze chemical residues. Other investigators included counterterrorism experts, forensic specialists, and psychological profilers, who began brainstorming motives behind the attack.

Visual examination of the 20-foot-wide (6.1m), 8-foot-deep (2.4m) crater led experts to believe that the bomb weighed between 1,000 and 2,000 pounds (453.6kg to 907.2kg) and was composed of an ammonium nitrate and fuel oil mixture known as ANFO. This was the same mixture that had been

An ATF agent searches for evidence near the Oklahoma City bomb site.

FBI agents at the site of the Oklahoma City bombing.

used in the World Trade Center bombing in 1993, and the materials were easily obtained for commercial and industrial purposes virtually anywhere in the United States. That left a wide array of suspects to track down. It was the job of the profilers to come up with theories as to what kind of person could be responsible.

Three theories emerged as to who could have committed the crime, based on what was known at the time. One theory, which was abandoned fairly early, was that gangs connected to Latin American drug cartels lashed out in revenge against the DEA, which had offices in the building. These cartels had been known to carry out bombings against rival factions and law enforcement targets, but never on the massive scale of Oklahoma City and never inside the United States. The ability of such a group to carry out this operation seemed a stretch, and the choice of the target seemed too random to make any sense. There were DEA offices in many other cities and several in Latin America that would have made better targets than the office in relatively remote Oklahoma City.

The second theory involved an attack by the radical right in the United States. Some investigators drew an immediate connection to this theory in that the date of the bombing was the second anniversary of the fire at the Branch Davidian compound in Waco, Texas. This was also the day that Richard Snell, a neo-Nazi revered in white supremacist circles, was scheduled to be executed.

The third theory, that the bombing was committed by Islamic terrorists from the Middle East, seemed the most plausible to investigators for a number of reasons. The style of the attack was almost identical to the 1993 World Trade Center bombing, and the choice of target was in the mode by which

A 20-foot-wide, 8-foot-deep crater was created by the bomb at the Murrah building in downtown Oklahoma City.

Richard Snell: Neo-Nazi Inspiration

Richard Snell had a long history of criminal activity associated with his involvement with the radical right that made him a hero among his colleagues in the white supremacist movement in the United States. His notoriety is detailed in Mark S. Hamm's book *In Bad Company:*

> The Internal Revenue Service had taken Snell to court over unpaid back taxes, and his property was seized by FBI agents from Oklahoma City. In October 1983 Snell [was] seeking assistance in implementing a revenge attack—on the Alfred P. Murrah federal building. The plan never materialized, but . . . Snell successfully committed two homicides and was involved in unsuccessful plots to assassinate a federal judge and to bomb a natural gas pipeline and an electrical transmission tower.

> Snell's plan to bomb the Murrah building was known by McVeigh, and this aided in McVeigh's selection of the building as a target.
> Snell was captured and convicted in 1985 and sentenced to die in an Arkansas state prison. He continued to communicate his antigovernment ideas through a newsletter he produced, and in the days leading up to his death, Snell told fellow inmates and guards that "justice is coming." He was executed on schedule on April 19, 1995, the same day as the Oklahoma City bombing.

Mark S. Hamm, *In Bad Company: America's Terrorist Underground.* Boston: Northeastern University Press, 2002, p. 112.

Islamic radicals operated. The Murrah building was a low-security federal installation in a city with a sizable Islamic population. Islamic terrorists had been carrying out attacks on Americans overseas for years, and after 1993 it was clear that they were looking to bring their war to American shores.

Whether individual investigators put more credence behind one theory or another, all avenues were explored. In line with the theory regarding Islamic terrorists, a man named Ibrahim Ahmad was taken into custody at Chicago's O'Hare International Airport. Ahmad matched the profile of possible suspects based on eyewitness accounts of Middle Eastern men in the vicinity of the Murrah building near the time of the bombing. Ahmad was a naturalized citizen of Palestinian descent who taught Arabic at an Oklahoma mosque. He was also traveling to the Middle East alone, which is a major signal to customs officials during a time of heightened security.

Ahmad was questioned for three hours by FBI agents, but was allowed to leave the country after the interview. Having missed his earlier flight to Rome, he flew to London with the intention of catching a flight from there to Amman, Jordan. However, Ahmad's luggage landed at Leonardo da Vinci Airport in Rome, where it was searched by Italian authorities at the request of the U.S. State Department. Mark Hamm notes in *Apocalypse in Oklahoma* what was discovered: "One bag contained a set of needle-nose pliers, a tube of silicon, and three jogging suits. A second bag held six kitchen knives, aluminum foil, black electrical tape, two spools of electrical wire, a camera, a video recorder, and a photograph album

By the Numbers

Oklahoma City Bombing Casualty Report

73
Age of oldest victim, Charles E. Hurlburt

4 MONTHS
Age of youngest victim, Gabreon Bruce

850
People injured

85
Rescuers injured

30
Children orphaned

219
Children who lost at least one parent

Source: Oklahoma City National Memorial. www.oklahomacity nationalmemorial.org/hist.htm.

with pictures of military weapons, including missiles and armored tanks."[12] Based on this suspicious assortment of travel gear, the federal government requested that authorities in London detain Ahmad upon his arrival at Heathrow Airport.

Another lead uncovered that day brought a significant break in the case. In the bomb squad's search for clues, investigators discovered the Ryder truck's 250-pound axle (113.4kg) about 400 feet (121.9m) away from the Murrah building. The force of the explosion had pitched it into the air, and it had landed on top of a red Ford Festiva, demolishing the automobile. They located the vehicle identification number (VIN) on the axle. The VIN is a seventeen-character code that is stamped on automobile parts, indicating the make, model, and

Investigators discovered the Ryder truck's 250-pound axle about 400 feet away from the Murrah building.

Gathering materials related to the 04.19.95 bombing continues to be an ongoing process for the Memorial in its effort to preserve every aspect of the incident. This license plate is from the rental truck driven by Timothy McVeigh. It was gathered by the FBI as part of the evidentiary material for use in the trials.
Artifact on loan from Federal Bureau of Investigation

manufacturer of all cars and trucks sold in the United States. By running the number through the FBI's Rapid Start System computer database, the investigators were able to determine the make and ownership.

Three hours later it was learned that the axle belonged to a 1993 Ford truck owned by a Ryder rental agency in Miami, Florida, and assigned for rental by Elliott's Body Shop in Junction City, Kansas, 270 miles (434.5km) north of Oklahoma City. FBI agents immediately set out for Junction City, hoping to learn just who had rented the truck and what his or her motivation was for committing cold-blooded mass murder on American soil.

Here is the license plate from the Ryder truck used to blow up the Murrah building.

CHAPTER 2

The Suspects

The violence and horror of the bombing of the Alfred P. Murrah federal building in Oklahoma City shocked the nation, and an outpouring of sympathy and material support flowed into the stricken city from across America. The rescue operation, which continued into the night of April 19, was buoyed by the arrival of firefighters and rescue personnel from around the state and other parts of the country. The criminal investigation, which was under the control of the FBI, had been categorized as a "major special," which means that bureau offices across the country and around the world had turned their attention to the case, now known internally as OKBOMB.

Many investigators wanted to explore the Islamic extremist angle. Islamic terrorists were the most plausible perpetrators because the style of the bombing matched the 1993 World Trade Center attack, and authorities already had a suspect in Ibrahim Ahmad, who was on a plane to London where U.S. authorities were waiting to bring him back to Washington for additional questioning. However, some officials thought otherwise.

Special agent Clinton Van Zandt of the FBI's Behavioral Science Unit in Quantico, Virginia, was drawn to the date of the bombing and thought it an important clue. Van Zandt spent many years studying the psychology of criminals for the bureau, and was its chief negotiator during the Branch Davidian siege in 1993. He believed that April 19, the second anniversary of the fire that killed seventy-five people, was a motivator for the bomber.

Van Zandt told his colleagues, "You're going to have a white male, acting alone or with one other person. He'll be in his mid-twenties. He'll have military experience and be a fringe

Investigators carefully sift through the rubble at the Murrah federal building bomb site.

member of some militia group. He'll be angry at the government for what happened at Ruby Ridge and Waco."[13]

Van Zandt was not the only law enforcement officer to draw a connection to the date of the bombing and the Waco tragedy, but many officials questioned the ability of an American militia group to have the expertise or resources to execute such a large attack.

Following the Middle Eastern Terrorist Lead

While the theory of American extremists carrying out an attack like that in Oklahoma City seemed far-fetched, the idea that Middle Eastern radicals were responsible for the bombing was very believable. Middle Eastern terrorists were known to have the resources and the expertise to carry out such a devastating attack and had done so in the past. The 1983 attack on the U.S. Marines barracks in Beirut, Lebanon, and the December 21, 1988, bombing of a Pan American airliner that killed 270, including 189 Americans, were examples of their ability to commit murder on a large scale. Also, eyewitnesses reported seeing Middle Eastern men rushing from the scene in the moments prior to the explosion that destroyed the Murrah building.

Jayna Davis, an award-winning investigative reporter who covered the Oklahoma City bombing, writes of one such eyewitness in her book *The Third Terrorist*. Manuel Acosta, on the morning of April 19, "observed a Middle Eastern man waving a hand signal to a foreign looking male who was standing on the north side of 5th Street. Both individuals were dark-complexioned with black hair. One man wore blue jogging pants, a black shirt and black jacket."[14] They took off in a brown Chevrolet pickup just minutes before the bomb went off. Other eyewitnesses also recall seeing the brown pickup and this pair of men.

Ahmad, who initially had been allowed to leave the country after he was interviewed by federal authorities in Chicago, was again a suspect when it was learned that among other incriminating items in his luggage was a jogging suit fitting the description given by Acosta and others. As soon as he landed in London, British authorities turned him over to the FBI agents, who promptly brought him back to Washington, D.C., for further questioning.

Ahmad was interrogated for two days by investigators who learned that he was a computer technician who had emigrated from Jordan to the United States on a student visa in 1982. Ahmad told the FBI that he had traveled to Jordan in early 1995 to visit his family, and because of a family emergency he was in the process of returning there on April 19 when he was stopped in Chicago.

While the FBI checked into Ahmad's background, two Pakistani men were picked up for questioning. Onis Siddiqi and his brother Assad were taken into custody in Dallas and Oklahoma City, respectively, where authorities asked them if they had any knowledge of the bombing. "They were asking

Ibrahim Ahmad, who was wrongly detained following the Oklahoma City bombing, reads a statement on November 9, 1995, outside the federal court in Oklahoma City.

me about my brother, my political affiliation," Onis told the *New York Times*. "They wanted to know what were my religious beliefs."[15]

A search of Onis Siddiqi's apartment in Dallas found no incriminating evidence and he passed a lie detector test. It turned out that the two brothers had traveled to Dallas and to Oklahoma City to deal with an immigration paperwork problem. They were subsequently released.

Ahmad was also released after his own story was confirmed with authorities. At this point, a significant lead had developed in the investigation that led federal investigators in a new—and startling—direction.

American Terrorists

While the interrogations of Ahmad and the Siddiqi brothers were taking place, a number of other FBI agents had descended

Flames engulf the Branch Davidian compound on April 19, 1993. The Oklahoma City bombing took place on the two-year anniversary of this event.

on Elliott's Body Shop in Junction City, Kansas, where the Ryder truck used in the bombing had been rented. A check of the rental records showed that the truck was rented by a Robert Kling of Redfield, South Dakota, on Monday, April 17. Kling's driver's license had an issue date of April 19, 1993, which was the date of the fire at the Branch Davidian compound in Waco, Texas. His date of birth was listed as April 19, 1970. The clerk at Elliott's Body Shop also told the FBI agents that the man who rented the truck and his companion were definitely white Americans. This information, combined with Van Zandt's theory about the significance of the date of April 19, suddenly changed the tempo of the investigation.

Experts from the FBI's Investigative and Prosecutive Graphics Unit made sketches of the two men based on descriptions given by the clerk and other employees. These drawings, known as composite sketches, are among the first tools used by law enforcement officers in trying to establish the identity of a potential suspect. A typical composite sketch will portray the

Experts from the FBI made sketches of the two suspects based on descriptions given by the clerk and other employees at Elliott's Body Shop.

The National Crime Information Center

As described on the Federal Bureau of Investigation's Web site:

> The National Crime Information Center (NCIC) is a computerized database of documented criminal justice information available to virtually every law enforcement agency nationwide, 24 hours a day, 365 days a year. The NCIC became operational on January 27, 1967, with the goal of assisting law enforcement in apprehending fugitives and locating stolen property. This goal has since expanded to include locating missing persons and further protecting law enforcement personnel and the public.
>
> This database has helped law enforcement agencies across the country solve a large number of crimes. It was also instrumental in locating Timothy McVeigh when the FBI sought him in connection with the Oklahoma City bombing.
>
> It is constantly updated by local, state, and federal law enforcement authorities with the latest information relating to crimes committed anywhere in the United States and its territories.

Federal Bureau of Investigation. www.fbi.gov/hq/cjisd/ncic_brochure.htm.

face of the person in question as described by an eyewitness and contain pertinent information such as height, weight, eye and hair color, what the person was wearing, and any scars or tattoos that may be visible in casual dress. The sketch is then circulated among other officers and distributed in the area where the suspect may have been seen.

FBI agents spent much of April 20 combing the streets of Junction City and interviewing business owners and citizens about the two men, now referred to as John Doe Number 1 and

John Doe Number 2. As noted in Hamm's *Apocalypse in Oklahoma,* "John Doe 1 was described as about 5 feet 10 inches tall, of medium build, weighing about 180 pounds, with light brown hair, and possibly right-handed. John Doe 2 was . . . about 5 feet 9 inches tall, weighing about 175 pounds, with brown hair, and a tattoo on his lower left arm."[16] Both were believed to be armed and extremely dangerous. And several people recalled seeing men resembling the suspects in and around Junction City in the days and weeks leading up to the bombing.

Gas station attendants, convenience store proprietors, and fast-food employees all noted their presence, many thinking they were soldiers from the nearby Fort Riley military installation. A salesman at an army-navy store called Fatigues and Things recalled John Doe 1 purchasing a handbook on making explosives titled *Improvised Munitions Manual.* When the sketches were shown to Lea McGown, owner of the Dreamland Motel on Interstate 70 leading out of Junction City, she identified John Doe 1 immediately.

A man matching that description had stayed at the Dreamland from April 14 to April 18, registering under the name Tim McVeigh and giving an address of 3616 North Van Dyke Road, Decker, Michigan. This was the second name attributed to John Doe 1, but it was likely the same person identified as Robert Kling by the employees at Elliott's Body Shop, because during the last two days of his stay McVeigh was driving a twenty-foot Ryder rental truck.

McGown was very clear about the details she gave the FBI agents. She remembered McVeigh distinctly for his neat appearance and pleasant manner and that he had haggled with her over the cost of his stay, which he paid in cash. He had arrived in a run-down yellow Mercury Marquis sedan with an Arizona license plate that was dangling from the bumper. And once he had rented the Ryder truck, McGown never again saw the Mercury.

With the Robert Kling identity leading to a dead end, federal authorities were now intent on tracking down McVeigh.

Agents were immediately dispatched to the Michigan address he had given McGown, and the hunt for the bombers entered an accelerated phase.

Apprehending Timothy McVeigh

As the evidence started to come together, the bulk of the FBI's resources shifted away from the Middle Eastern terrorist theory and began to focus on the troubling prospect that the bombing was the work of Americans. While John Doe Number 2 remained unidentified, authorities were sure that John Doe Number 1 was Timothy McVeigh and that he had played a significant role in the bombing.

McVeigh's name was plugged into the national crime database maintained by the FBI's National Crime Information Center in an effort to learn more about him and any other crimes he may have committed in the past. As it turned out, McVeigh was already in custody for a misdemeanor weapons violation in a Noble County, Oklahoma, jail. The agents had to act fast because McVeigh was about to make bail and be released.

Timothy McVeigh had been stopped at 10:30 a.m. on April 19 outside the town of Perry, sixty miles north of Oklahoma City, for not having a license plate on his car, a yellow 1977 Mercury Marquis. The highway patrolman who pulled him over noticed a bulge under his jacket, and McVeigh admitted that he was armed with a .45-caliber Glock pistol. He was promptly arrested and taken to the Noble County Sheriff's Department where he waited to be arraigned on charges of carrying a concealed weapon, transporting a loaded weapon, and driving without a license plate or insurance.

On Friday, April 21, McVeigh was to due to appear before the county judge, and he would be released on a five-thousand-dollar bond, his court appearance to be scheduled for a later date. While McVeigh was waiting to post bond, FBI agents contacted Sheriff Jerry Cook and told him McVeigh was the prime suspect in the Oklahoma City bombing. McVeigh's court appearance was stalled until federal agents arrived at the jail and interviewed him. The session yielded no new information from McVeigh, who remained calm and refused to say anything without first talking to a lawyer.

Since it was now clear that it was McVeigh who had rented the truck used in the bombing, investigators were confident about taking him into custody. A search of his car, which matched McGown's description of the vehicle he drove in Junction City, turned up a large envelope that included antigovernment literature and newspaper clippings of the siege at Waco two years earlier. FBI agents dispatched to McVeigh's hometown of Pendleton, New York, in an effort to learn about his background, spoke with Carl Lebron Jr., a colleague of McVeigh's when he worked as a security guard years before. Lebron added more weight to McVeigh's views about Waco.

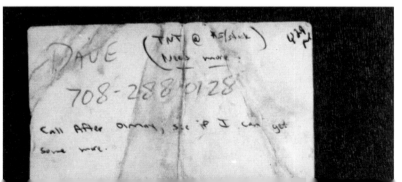

This business card, found in the backseat of the Oklahoma state trooper's patrol car after he arrested Timothy McVeigh, was entered into evidence in McVeigh's trial.

Lou Michel and Dan Herbeck, two staff reporters for the *Buffalo News*, investigated the Oklahoma City Bombing, making note of Lebron's conversation with the FBI in their book *American Terrorist: Timothy McVeigh and the Oklahoma City Bombing*. "Lebron told the agents about McVeigh's extremist political views, and his rage over the deaths at Waco. He mentioned that McVeigh had visited Waco to protest. He also turned over a photo of McVeigh, a Waco videotape, and some antigovernment pamphlets McVeigh had given him—along with an address McVeigh had used in Kingman, AZ."[17]

The misdemeanor charges against McVeigh were dropped as a legal formality so that he could be released by the Noble County Sheriff's Department and placed in the custody of the FBI. By the time he was to be transported to Oklahoma City to be charged with the bombing, a large crowd had gathered outside the courthouse. Informed by the media that the prime suspect was inside, angry Oklahomans shouted "baby killer," "coward," and obscenities as McVeigh was led to a helicopter that took him to Tinker Air Force Base. He was charged on April 21, 1995, "under Title 18 of U.S. Code, Section 844, with 'malicious danger and destroying by means of an explosive' a federal building."[18]

However, the FBI's work was not finished. John Doe Number 2 was still unidentified and at large. And the investigation was simultaneously expanding further in Decker, Michigan.

The Nichols Brothers

The Michigan address McVeigh gave to McGown when registering at the Dreamland Motel was a farm owned by James Nichols and, as with McVeigh, federal authorities wanted to learn everything they could about him. While McVeigh was being turned over to federal custody, FBI and ATF agents performed a raid on Nichols's home.

While Nichols was questioned about his possible involvement in the bombing and his ties to McVeigh, an extensive search of his property turned up a quantity of diesel fuel, fertilizer, rifles, and blasting caps, which are small devices used to ignite an explosive. While it is not unusual to find fuel and fertilizer on a farm, agents were curious about Nichols's involvement in the Michigan Militia, an antigovernment group,

FBI and ATF agents search the house and property of James Nichols.

and the profile created of him based on interviews with neighbors and associates. According to them, Nichols was an ardent supporter of right-wing views and had been known to detonate explosives on his property. His ex-wife, Kelli Padilla, informed the FBI that McVeigh had stayed at the farm a number of times over the previous two years, along with Nichols's brother, Terry. Terry's ex-wife, Lana Padilla, who is Kelli's sister, corroborated this information. This led the authorities to the home of Terry Nichols in Herington, Kansas, some twenty-five miles (40.2km) from Junction City.

Gathering Evidence

The FBI knew little about the nature of Nichols's association with McVeigh, but the fact that they spent time together in Michigan was enough to bring Nichols in for questioning. Oddly, it was Nichols who came to the authorities on Friday afternoon after he heard his name on television and radio reports in connection with the Oklahoma City bombing.

FBI agents questioned Nichols extensively, and even though he claimed to have no knowledge of the bombing, he provided a wealth of information. Relying on a tried and true interrogation tactic to "keep them talking," agents befriended Nichols, pumping him with questions about his association with McVeigh, allowing his answers to lead to more questions and yet more answers. They discovered that Nichols had met McVeigh when both men were serving in the U.S. Army and that they had remained friends after they were both discharged. It also became clear that Nichols had spent time with McVeigh in the months and weeks leading up to the bombing. After a few hours of questioning, however, Nichols was contradicting his own earlier statements about certain times he was supposedly with McVeigh.

During searches of Nichols's home, agents found

five 6-foot cords with nonelectric blasting caps, one fuel meter, and several containers of ground ammoni-

The Michigan Militia

The Michigan Militia was formed in 1994 by Norman Olson of Alanson, Michigan, in response to the federal government's tightening of gun control laws in the United States. The militia described itself as a group dedicated to informing, training, and promoting defense among citizens who share a knowledge and respect for firearms.

At its height during the mid-1990s, the militia boasted some ten thousand members who were organized into regiments structured after the U.S. Army, with four regional commands around the state of Michigan. Meetings and weekend training missions were held, during which people would gather to discuss their fears of a federal government that was unfairly taxing its citizens and treating law-abiding gun owners as criminals.

James and Terry Nichols were among the more radical members of the militia, which came under FBI scrutiny after the Oklahoma City bombing. Olson vehemently denounced the bombing and denied that the militia or anyone in it played a role. Many of the group's radical members were expelled, and the organization was eventually cleared of any involvement in the bombing. Enrollment declined sharply in the late 1990s, and the Michigan Militia faded into obscurity.

um nitrate. They also found four white barrels with blue lids made from material resembling the blue plastic fragments found at the bomb scene, 33 firearms and an anti-tank weapon, plus numerous books, pamphlets and brochures dealing with the Waco siege, tax protests and anti-government warfare.[19]

Another important item found was a receipt for the purchase of 2,000 pounds (907kg) of ammonium nitrate. FBI forensics experts analyzed the receipt for fingerprints. Fingerprinting is an exact science with a 100 percent probability of

Crime Scene Search, Record, and Physical Evidence Collection

This standardized process for searching a crime scene represents the protocol followed by FBI agents in their search of James Nichols's Michigan farm and Terry Nichols's home in Herington, Kansas.

1 **Use** a search pattern.

2 **Search from the general to the specific** for evidence, and be alert for all evidence.

3 **Search entrances** and exits.

4 **Photograph all items** before collection and mark evidence locations on a sketch. Note all evidence in the evidence log.

5 **Wear latex or cotton gloves** to avoid leaving fingerprints. Do not excessively handle the evidence after recovery.

6 **Seal all evidence packages** at the crime scene.

7 **Make a complete evaluation** of the crime scene.

8 **Discuss the search** with all personnel.

9 **Ensure all documentation** is correct and complete.

10 **Photograph the scene** showing the final condition.

11 **Ensure all evidence** is secured.

accuracy because no two people can have the same set of fingerprints. These prints, made by the unique raised ridges of skin on a person's fingertips and palms, are frequently used as a form of identification, which is the reason they are collected whenever a person is arrested. Prints help determine if that person was present at a crime scene or if they handled any items used in committing a crime. There are three basic parts of a fingerprint that can identify it with a particular person—the arch at the very tip of the finger; the loop, which is just below the arch; and the whorl, which runs under the loop.

In the case of the receipt, the forensics team examined the paper for latent, or invisible, prints. Even if a person's fingerprint cannot be seen with the naked eye, sweat secretions from their skin will leave a residue that can be identified through chemical analysis. This analysis raises, or makes visible, the print. By comparing the prints on the receipt with the fingerprints taken from Nichols and McVeigh, it was determined that both men had handled the receipt.

These prints, along with the explosives and chemicals found at the homes of James and Terry Nichols, provided enough evidence to hold both men as material witnesses in the case, meaning that their testimony would be necessary for trial. Although no one could place James or Terry Nichols in Oklahoma City at the time of the bombing, it was clear that they could provide more information in the investigation.

Placing McVeigh at the Scene of the Crime

The work of FBI field agents in Junction City, Kansas, led investigators to determine without a doubt that McVeigh had rented the truck that was used in the bombing. This was significant, but they still could not precisely determine if he drove the truck to the Murrah building and ignited the fuse that set off the bomb. They would be assisted in this by a closer examination of the crime scene.

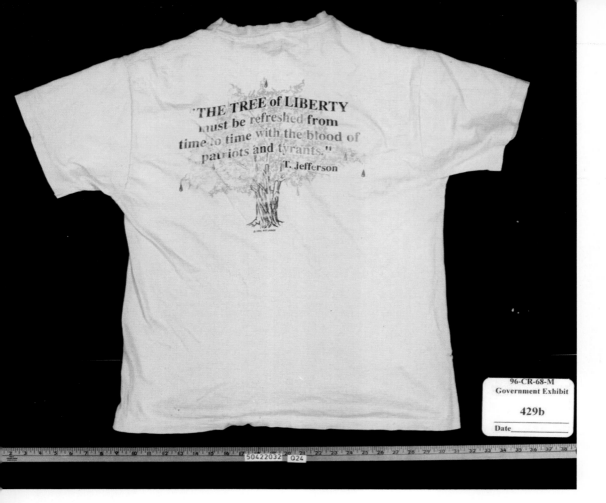

Traces of an explosive used in bomb detonators were detected on the shirt that Timothy McVeigh was wearing when he was arrested.

Explosives experts examining the bomb crater in the days following the bombing discovered trace elements of chemicals that were foreign to the area, meaning that these chemicals were not present prior to the bombing. Soil samples and 7,000 pounds (3,175.2kg) of debris were shipped in sealed evidence pouches to the crime laboratory at FBI headquarters in Washington, D.C., for analysis. By examining the soil and debris in chemical tests and with powerful electron microscopes, scientists confirmed the theory that the bomb was composed of a mixture of ammonium nitrate and nitromethane (ANFO), a volatile, or highly combustible, fuel used in auto racing. It was further determined that the mixture was lit with a slow-burning fuse attached to a detonating cord that ignited an explosive batch of Tovex. Tovex, a blasting gelatin used in mining and demolition, was used here as a booster, or primer charge, to set off the ANFO mix.

The clothing that McVeigh was wearing on April 19 was also sent to the FBI lab for analysis, and trace elements of the chemicals used in the bomb were discovered. This determined that McVeigh was in or near the Ryder truck after the bomb was

Fiber Analysis

The analysis of Timothy McVeigh's clothing for traces of the explosive used in the bomb that destroyed the Murrah building followed a strict procedure used by forensic scientists to connect suspects to criminal acts. When someone handles explosives, traces of the explosive chemicals can be found in their clothing, but only careful analysis of the fibers will yield results.

1 **Sample preparation:** Visual inspection of the material with magnifiers or microscopes

2 **Source determination:** Establish if the sample came from victim, suspect, or scene

3 **Physical characteristics:** Establish size, color, shape, and manufacture

4 **Various testing procedures:** Heat solubility, light refraction, and magnification to detect specific chemicals that would not ordinarily be found in clothing fibers

Source:"Forensic Fiber Examination Guidelines," *Forensic Science Communications*, vol. 1, no. 1, April 1999. www.fbi.gov/hq/lab/fsc/backissu/april 1999/houckch2.htm#7.0.Analysis.

loaded. However, McVeigh's clothes were not shipped or stored in a sealed pouch to prevent contamination. They were shipped in a brown paper sack, which allowed them to be exposed to other chemicals and would call into question the validity of the analysis. Whenever items are meant to be examined for chemical or material analysis, they must be transported and stored in sealed evidence bags that are clearly labeled, otherwise the items run the risk of being contaminated by other chemicals or particles. This can ruin a piece of evidence, making it unusable in court and consequently affecting the entire case.

The explosives report, which was released by the FBI crime lab on September 5, 1995, also contained a questionable finding about the size of the bomb. Investigators concluded that

Michael Fortier, a friend of Timothy McVeigh and Terry Nichols, was sentenced to twelve years in prison for knowing about the bomb plot and not telling authorities.

the bomb weighed approximately 5,000 pounds (2268kg), twice as large as originally estimated. This scientific conclusion should have been reached solely by studying the building's structural damage, the chemical makeup of the bomb, and the size of the crater. However, the conclusion was reached in part because of the purchase receipts for ammonium nitrate found at Terry Nichols's residence.

Several complaints about the research procedures in the FBI's crime lab in this and other criminal investigations motivated the Office of the Inspector General (OIG) in the Department of Justice to begin an inquiry into the lab in the fall of 1995. This did not dissuade authorities from continuing their work in solving the case. Agents searched for clues in Oklahoma, New York, Michigan, Kansas, and Arizona, where another man, Michael Fortier, was also taken into custody. Fortier, a hardware store employee living in Kingman, Arizona, had served in the army with McVeigh and Nichols. McVeigh had also stayed with him a number of times over the last two years, and was the best man at his wedding. Fortier shared the same right-wing views as McVeigh, who had used a Kingman address to receive mail. Fortier admitted to the FBI that he helped McVeigh and Nichols transport stolen weapons and, after he was told that he could face the death penalty for his connection to the bombing, agreed to be a witness for the prosecution.

With the evidence collected against McVeigh, Fortier, and the Nichols brothers, the FBI realized that Americans were responsible for the bombing and dismissed the theory regarding Middle Eastern terrorists. But why would a small group of men commit such a heinous crime against their fellow citizens? Why would they pick a federal office building in Oklahoma City as their target? How far did the conspiracy reach? And would there be more attacks?

The answers would be found in piecing together the life and travels of McVeigh, the man who had become the prime suspect in the Oklahoma City bombing.

CHAPTER 3

On the Trail of Mass Murderers

The clues that led to the arrests of McVeigh, the Nichols brothers, and Fortier were just the beginning of the investigation into their lives and backgrounds. Many questions still had to be answered by federal authorities in order to successfully prosecute a case. Relying on evidence that McVeigh had rented the Ryder truck and been in close proximity to the bomb, investigators made him the focus of that case.

In the court of public opinion, McVeigh was already guilty. A May 1, 1995, *Time* magazine cover story called him "The Face of Terror," and this title summed up the national consensus that McVeigh was an unholy monster. Indeed, it took a diabolical mind to think up, plan, and execute the most devastating terrorist attack perpetrated on American soil up to that time. However, prosecutors cannot rely on public opinion to prove their case. They must present tangible evidence that proves the guilt of the defendant beyond a reasonable doubt. The search for that evidence started in learning more about McVeigh and his associates.

The government's investigation of McVeigh was one of the most extensive the U.S. Justice Department has ever undertaken. Thousands of hours of interviews were conducted with family members, boyhood friends, work associates, and colleagues from the military. It was also hoped that clues could be found as to the motive behind his actions, as well as the roles he and his accomplices may have played in carrying out the bombing.

The Survivalist

FBI agents descended on McVeigh's hometown of Pendleton, New York, the day he became the prime suspect in the bombing. In an effort to gather information about his life, they conducted dozens of interviews with several of McVeigh's high school classmates and work colleagues as well as with his father, Bill. After conducting each interview the agents filed a report called a 302. These 302s were then collected and analyzed by profilers who assembled a biography of McVeigh that would yield clues about what motivated him to commit the attack on the Murrah building.

It was apparent that McVeigh was a survivalist from an early age. A survivalist is someone who habitually prepares for disaster, natural or otherwise, by learning such skills as emergency medical training, hunting, and self-defense and by stockpiling food, water, and sometimes weapons. Born Timothy James McVeigh on April 23, 1968, in the suburbs of Buffalo, New York, he modeled himself after his paternal grandfather, Edward, who kept barrels of water, canned food, guns, and ammunition in his basement in case of emergencies. Edward gave McVeigh a .22 rifle when he was nine years old, thus beginning McVeigh's lifelong affinity for firearms.

McVeigh's parents, Bill and Mildred, divorced in 1984 when he was sixteen, and his sisters Patty and Jennifer moved with their mother to Florida, while he remained with his father in Pendleton. Interviews with McVeigh's former teachers revealed that he maintained good grades throughout high school, stayed out of

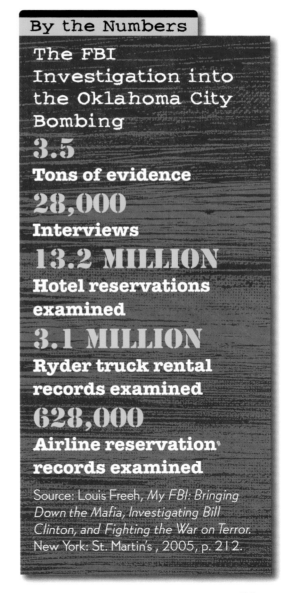

By the Numbers

The FBI Investigation into the Oklahoma City Bombing

3.5
Tons of evidence

28,000
Interviews

13.2 MILLION
Hotel reservations examined

3.1 MILLION
Ryder truck rental records examined

628,000
Airline reservation records examined

Source: Louis Freeh, *My FBI: Bringing Down the Mafia, Investigating Bill Clinton, and Fighting the War on Terror.* New York: St. Martin's, 2005, p. 212.

trouble, and did not drink alcohol or smoke. He rarely dated, and he was thought of by his classmates as friendly but reserved. After graduating from high school in 1986, McVeigh spent an unproductive semester in business school, but, according to his father, he was aimless and faced a life with no prospects.

At this point McVeigh began to exhibit traits that piqued the curiosity of the FBI investigators. McVeigh's reading list

William Pierce, Author of *The Turner Diaries*

William Pierce, born September 11, 1933, was a physics professor at Oregon State University when he became involved in George Lincoln Rockwell's American Nazi Party in 1966. Although Pierce possessed a keen intellect, he had harbored racist views all of his life. He believed the civil rights movement and the antiwar movement of the 1960s to be inspired by Communists and a threat to the white race.

After Rockwell's death, Pierce created his own white supremacist group, the National Alliance, which was based in West Virginia. Through radio programs, lectures, and literature, Pierce communicated his view of white racial purity and the threat posed to it by minorities and Jews. His philosophy, which he maintained was Christian in nature, had strong religious underpinnings but was heavily influenced by Adolf Hitler's theories about Aryan superiority.

In 1978 Pierce wrote *The Turner Diaries,* a fictional tale about a race war in which white Aryans overthrow the U.S. government. The book and Pierce's teachings are believed to be responsible for inspiring not only Timothy McVeigh's attack on the Murrah building, but other acts of violence committed by white supremacist groups.

Pierce died on July 23, 2002.

expanded from magazines like *Soldier of Fortune* and *Guns &
Ammo* to materials about the antigovernment extreme right.
One book that significantly impacted his thinking was *The
Turner Diaries*, written by William Pierce, an ardent white supremacist and former high-ranking member of the American
Nazi Party. Although a work of racist fiction, the FBI knew
the book was heralded as a manifesto by right-wing extremists, gun enthusiasts, and antigovernment protestors. It told
the story of a group of white supremacists who start a revolution against the U.S. government. At one point the book's hero,
Earl Turner, uses a truck bomb to destroy the FBI headquarters in Washington, D.C.

McVeigh wholly absorbed the book's advocacy of gun
rights, and many of the people interviewed by FBI agents noted that he was never without a copy. He freely offered copies
to friends in an effort to stir their feelings about government
intrusion into private lives. He also applied for a pistol per-
mit which allowed him to obtain a job as a security guard with
Burke Armored Car Service.

At Burke, McVeigh was considered a good employee, but
his coworkers grew uneasy about his zealous survivalist views.
Coworker Jeff Camp remembers one time when "McVeigh
showed up at work in camouflage clothing and crossed ban-
doliers of ammunition. It was another joke, this one played on
a supervisor, but it made a lasting impression at Burke."[20]

With money saved from his job, McVeigh collected more
guns, and in April 1988 he and a friend purchased a 10-acre tract
(4ha) of land, which they set up as a firing range. Research into
the New York state police records of that time revealed that a
formal complaint had been lodged against McVeigh about the
excessive amounts of gunfire. The report indicated that "it sound-
ed like bombs were being set off on the property."[21]

McVeigh's survivalist tendencies, his love of firearms, and
his absorption of antigovernment literature fit the FBI profile
of someone who could be categorized as a right-wing extremist. His term of service in the army was of particular interest

to investigators, however, because it provided him with an opportunity to expand his knowledge of firearms and acquire an extensive knowledge of explosives.

The Conspirators

McVeigh signed up for a three-year enlistment in the U.S. Army on May 24, 1988. Examination of his army file and FBI interviews with his basic training drill instructors at Fort Benning, Georgia, and from his commanding officers at Fort Riley, Kansas, indicated that he was a model soldier. He thrived in the military environment of hard training, strict discipline, and attentive detail. However, he still clung to his antigovernment beliefs, and he found kindred spirits in two fellow recruits, Nichols and Fortier.

The FBI had discovered early in their investigation that these three men met in the army and were simultaneously researching the backgrounds of Nichols and Fortier in the same manner as McVeigh. Extensive interviews were conducted with family members, and employment records and bank accounts were searched. They learned that Nichols was thirty-three years old when he joined the army; an unusual step for a man his age, but his life up to that point had consisted of little more than a strained marriage, a string of failed business ventures, and an unhappy family background. Watching his family and other farmers in Michigan suffer what he believed to be unfair taxes and regulation, he grew to harbor a deep resentment of the federal government. He was often in debt and at one point even petitioned the courts in Michigan to renounce his citizenship in order to avoid paying his enormous credit card bills.

Fortier had enlisted in the army simply because military service was a family tradition. He lacked the discipline of McVeigh, and he enjoyed partying more than marching and drilling. But when McVeigh lent him a copy of *The Turner Diaries,* it left an indelible impression on Fortier.

Agents took note of the fact that McVeigh, Nichols, and Fortier had something in common—a shared negative view of

Becoming an FBI Agent

Job Description:
FBI special agents are responsible for conducting sensitive national security investigations and for enforcing over three hundred federal statutes. As an FBI special agent you may work on matters including terrorism, foreign counterintelligence, cyber-crime, organized crime, white-collar crime, public corruption, civil rights violations, financial crime, bribery, bank robbery, extortion, kidnapping, air piracy, interstate criminal activity, fugitive and drug-trafficking matters, and other violations of federal statutes.

Education:
Four-year degree from a college or university accredited by the U.S. secretary of education.

Qualifications:
All applicants must qualify for one of the Bureau's five entry programs—Accounting, Computer Science/Information Technology, Language, Law, or Diversified. After qualifying, applicants are prioritized based on certain critical skills the FBI is looking for, and these skills are based on demand. Intensive law, weapons, and physical training is also involved.

Additional Information:
The job of an FBI special agent is extremely rigorous but rewarding. Currently, the FBI is recruiting heavily to assign more agents to combating terrorism and Internet and computer crimes.

Salary:
Special Agents receive a starting salary of $43,705 while in the sixteen-week training program at the FBI academy located at Quantico, Virginia. Upon graduation, the salary ranges from $53,743 to $58,335 depending upon the locality pay of the geographic assignment.

Sources: Federal Bureau of Investigation, www.fbijobs.gov/111.asp, www.fbi.gov/pressrel/pressrel02/hire012302.htm.

the government. They had also all come to the military because they had no other options available in life. Profilers took notice that McVeigh seemed to stand out in his zeal and were increasingly confident that he was the ringleader of the Oklahoma City bombing plot. He was more vocal about his beliefs than either Nichols or Fortier, and his military skills exceeded not only that of his two friends but many of his fellow soldiers.

Army records revealed that in the spring of 1989 Nichols received a hardship discharge to take care of his son after his wife filed for divorce. Fortier was assigned light duty because of a shoulder injury. By contrast, McVeigh excelled in his duties, and he was assigned as a gunner of an armored troop transport known as a Bradley fighting vehicle. As part of his training, he practiced rifle marksmanship and learned how to handle, fire, and care for a variety of firearms. He also learned about ordnance and the components of rocket shells, grenades, and bombs. Commanding these skills was standard for any soldier, but McVeigh went above and beyond what was required. Some of his fellow soldiers thought he was overzealous. "He played the military twenty-four hours a day, seven days a week," said one crew member. "All of us thought it was silly. When they'd call for down time, we'd rest, and he'd throw on a rucksack and walk around the post with it."[22]

McVeigh's constant attention to his equipment and his duties may have driven his buddies crazy, but it paid off for him. He was promoted to sergeant in the fall of 1990, and he reenlisted for another three years. In December he was sent to Saudi Arabia as part of the massive American military buildup that preceded the Persian Gulf War.

Disillusionment and Anger

Based on a review of letters he sent home from Saudi Arabia, it was clear to investigators that McVeigh's service in the Persian Gulf War of 1991 was a sobering experience. His Bradley unit was part of the first wave of ground forces sent in to liberate the country of Kuwait from the forces of Iraqi leader Saddam Hussein. He felt bad for the Iraqi soldiers who surrendered in droves as the American forces approached. After weeks of aerial bombardment, much of the Iraqi occupying force had been decimated, and those who were left were often starved and frightened. McVeigh would say years later, "They were regular guys. I felt the army brainwashed us to hate them."[23]

McVeigh performed effectively during combat, and on March 3, when U.S. commanding general H. Norman Schwarzkopf signed the armistice with the commanders in Iraq, McVeigh was selected to be part of the security detail. When he returned to Fort Riley at the end of March 1991, McVeigh was ordered to report to the Special Forces Selection and Assessment Course at Fort Bragg, North Carolina.

McVeigh Resigns from the Army

Joining the Special Forces was an opportunity that McVeigh had dreamed of since childhood, and he had earned it with his exemplary service in the war. He received numerous awards for valor, courage, and conduct, but his body was fatigued from the months he had spent in the Persian Gulf. After just two days of grueling marches and fitness drills, he withdrew from the program. Without an opportunity to join the Special Forces, he felt there was nothing left for him that would equal the honor and duty of combat.

McVeigh returned to Fort Riley, but army life had become a drudgery for him. FBI 302s from interviews with his fellow soldiers revealed that he spent his time perusing the pawn shops and gun stores for new guns to buy and reading articles about the federal government's attempts at gun control in *Soldier of Fortune* and other publications. He grew despondent about serving a government that he had come to believe was stripping away individual rights, and on December 31, 1991, McVeigh resigned his army commission.

McVeigh returned to Pendleton and got a job at Burns Security in nearby Buffalo. He also joined the National Guard,

In a letter written by Timothy McVeigh to the Oklahoma Gazette *in November 1996, McVeigh blames the FBI for the 1993 deaths of 80 members of the Branch Davidian cult near Waco, Texas.*

but he was preoccupied with the idea that the federal government was seeking greater control over people's lives, a constant theme in antigovernment circles. Lebron, his colleague at Burns, remembers a lot of talk about "politics, secret societies, some religion and conspiracy theories."[24]

The FBI discovered letters McVeigh wrote to the *Lockport Union-Sun and Journal* in which he would complain about the ills of American society—crime, high taxes, and corrupt politicians. "What is it going to take to open the eyes of our elected officials?" He wrote in one such letter. "Do we have to shed blood to reform the current system? I hope it doesn't come to that! But it might."[25]

In December 1992 McVeigh quit his job at Burns Security and began traveling around the country. During this time his movements were difficult to track because he did not leave a

26 NOV 96

Phil,

After reading your most recent article ("Citizen McVeigh"), I am tempted to use it as a springboard to start correcting some of those "myths" that you mention. In the interest of brevity (and fearing the wrath of my attorneys), however, I will stick to a single issue.

I commend you for your excellent recall and your absolute fairness. (Now I know why you can't get a job at the Washington Post.) Your notes on one point, though, are slightly inaccurate. You quote me as saying that the FBI are "wizards at PR". What I actually said is that they are wizards of propaganda – which Webster's defines as "information or ideas methodically spread to promote or injure a cause." This is where I drew the parallel between the FBI's efforts in my case, and those at Waco.

The idea is that once the FBI can control the flow of information, they can then demonize their target. In my case, I have been sealed away in federal prison and denied most visitation and free communication.

At Waco, once the FBI blocked the Davidians abilities to communicate with the outside world, Bob Ricks could then step forward and mold the facts to fit the FBI's purposes. The public never saw the Davidians home videos of their cute babies, adorable children, loving mothers, or protective fathers. Nor did they see pictures of the charred remains of children's bodies. Therefore, they didn't c when these families died a slow, tortuous death as they were gassed and burned alive at the hands of the FBI. They didn't care when boastful FBI agents posed for the camera as people's lives were consumed in flame.

In both situations, as with Richard Jewell you only hear one side of the story, and it is usually not truthful. If you have trouble believing that the Justice Department are all liars – come to one of my pre-trial hearings, the trial itself, or ask Richard Jewell.

People need to question and analyze what they hear, and ponder the motivations of those spreading the propaganda. The truth lies deeper.

Thank You for your t

Tim

trail. Law enforcement can track a person's movements by examining bank statements to see when and where they may have used a credit card or by reviewing hotel registries to see where they may have stayed. But McVeigh paid cash wherever he went and often slept in his car or by the side of the road.

FBI agents learned from interviews with dealers at gun shows that McVeigh made money buying and selling guns, army surplus equipment, and copies of *The Turner Diaries*. "He carried that book all the time," a gun collector told the *New York Times*. "He sold it at the shows. He'd have a few copies in the cargo pocket of his cammies. They were supposed to be $10, but he'd sell them for $5. It was like he was looking for converts."[26]

It is known that in February 1993 McVeigh went to Decker, Michigan, to visit the Nichols brothers. He worked the farm with them, and they commiserated about politics and shot firearms for practice. After the Waco siege began later that month, McVeigh drove to Texas to join the scores of people protesting the government's actions there. He returned to Michigan after a few days, and when the fire ended the siege on April 19 he became extremely angry. As McVeigh and the Nichols brothers saw it, first the government came for Randy Weaver, then they came for the Branch Davidians. How long would it be before any of them, any citizen at all, would fall victim to the tyrannical forces in Washington?

McVeigh began taking a serious interest in explosives. The Waco tragedy was very much on his mind, and he talked about it with anyone who would listen. With the Nichols brothers he began building small bombs and exploding them in the fields. Police reports from this time reveal that James Nichols was the subject of numerous complaints about using explosives on his property. He also told McVeigh about Snell, the leader in the white supremacist movement who had once planned to blow up the Alfred P. Murrah federal building in Oklahoma City.

In February 1994 McVeigh drove to Kingman, Arizona, to visit Fortier and his longtime girlfriend, Lori Hart. Fortier, now a heavy user of illegal drugs, spent his time with a sordid group of people known by local police as "desert rats"—drug users and sellers who often engaged in petty crime to make ends meet. Fortier got McVeigh a job at the local hardware store. McVeigh continued to make the rounds at gun shows and he also kept up his avid reading, but now he was focused on information about explosive compounds and materials. He stayed in Arizona for a few months, serving as best man when Fortier married Hart in June.

When the assault weapons ban known as the Brady Bill became law on September 13, 1994, the news angered and terrified McVeigh. In reality the law was an attempt to rid the streets of the most dangerous firearms then legally available; guns that had been used in drug-related and gang violence had claimed the lives of young men in cities all over the country. To McVeigh and other right-wing extremists, it was just the latest step in a carefully crafted plan to disarm citizens before subjecting them to tyrannical government authority. The paranoid gun culture in which McVeigh had become absorbed believed that stricter laws would soon follow. As Michel and Herbeck write in *American Terrorist*, "To McVeigh, history was repeating itself. The federal government had become equated in his mind with the British government of pre-Revolutionary America. McVeigh could take no more."[27]

Acquiring the Tools for Mass Murder

The FBI's investigative work up to this point established McVeigh's motivation to commit the bombing in Oklahoma City. However, the hard evidence about the plot itself that would be needed to secure a conviction in court was still lacking. McVeigh's defense attorneys would surely point out that he was not the only man who held extremist views or harbored resentment over Waco. The gun show circuit was filled with people who talked about "doing something" to stop the encroaching power of the federal government, but few ever did. The FBI needed to prove that McVeigh not only talked, but acted.

Oklahoma City bombing conspirator Terry Nichols.

Beginning with the purchase receipt for 2,000 pounds (907kg) of ammonium nitrate found at Terry Nichols's house, agents were able to follow the chain of events that included gathering the materials necessary to build the bomb. The receipt, which had both Nichols's and McVeigh's fingerprints on it, was dated September 30, 1994, from the Mid-Kansas Cooperative Association in McPherson, Kansas. Reviews of sales records at the cooperative revealed that Nichols had used the alias Mike Havens and had made a second purchase of 2,000 pounds (907kg) of ammonium nitrate on October 18. Havens's true identity was determined when employees were shown a photograph of Nichols.

In questioning Nichols about other items found in his home, which included blasting caps and fuses, investigators

A photo of fifty-five-gallon plastic barrels that authorities believe were used in the construction of the bomb used in the Oklahoma City bombing.

learned that he and McVeigh had committed a robbery to acquire materials for the bomb. On October 3, 1994, they broke into the storage facility at the Martin Marietta Aggregates quarry in Marion, Kansas, and stole seven 50-pound boxes (22.7kg) of Tovex blasting gelatin, five hundred electric blasting caps, and eighty spools of ignition cord. Local police had noted that this robbery was reported, but up until now it remained unsolved.

Phone records became another indispensable resource to investigators in learning more about the acquisition of bomb-making materials. McVeigh often used telephone calling cards, sometimes purchased under his own name. An examination of calls made using these cards, as well as calls made from Fortier's home in Arizona, indicated that McVeigh contacted a number of businesses that sold plastic drums, composite explosive materials, and fuel oil.

Agents also discovered a network of storage lockers in Kansas, Arizona, and Las Vegas, Nevada, that were used by McVeigh and Nichols to store their materials. One storage locker in Kansas had been rented by McVeigh to store his growing collection of guns while he was at nearby Fort Riley. The other lockers were rented throughout the fall of 1994 under various aliases that had been traced and discovered by FBI investigators through examination of addresses, phone records, and physical descriptions that identified the suspects. These facilities were used to store ammonium nitrate, blasting caps, Tovex, and other bomb materials.

The discovery of the storage lockers and the trail of evidence that detailed the acquisition of materials to build the bomb made FBI investigators confident that along with McVeigh's motive, they also had enough hard evidence to convict him. From this point forward it would be the responsibility of federal prosecutors to present that evidence and to obtain a guilty verdict from a jury. Before that, though, they would be engaged in a number of pretrial maneuvers that threatened to derail the government's case.

CHAPTER 4

Pretrial Battles

After the capture of McVeigh, Fortier, and the Nichols brothers, the government's search for a wider conspiracy stalled. None of the investigators wanted to believe that such a destructive plot could be hatched by one or two men, but leads to other individuals went cold. On May 23, 1995, a federal court judge ruled that there was not enough evidence to continue holding James Nichols, and he was freed, pending trial. Charges linking him to the bombing were later dropped. The FBI had also called off the search for the elusive John Doe Number 2. They established the identity of the person represented in the composite sketch as Private Todd Bunting, a soldier stationed at Fort Riley near Junction City who had no connection to the bombing.

However, the chemical residues found on McVeigh's clothing and the explosive materials found at Terry Nichols's house convinced a federal judge that these two men should remain in custody and be held without bail. Fortier had agreed to be a witness for the prosecution, so he also remained in federal custody. At this point a great deal of legal maneuvering took place, as both the prosecution and the defense would do everything they could to achieve an advantage in the courtroom.

The Trial Teams Take Shape

Investigators in the field continued searching for clues that could concretely prove McVeigh's and Nichols's involvement in the bombing. FBI lab technicians and forensics experts also continued their work analyzing case evidence, which continued to pour in from the crime scene and from the searches of the Nichols brothers' homes. Meanwhile, the U.S. Justice

Department put together its prosecution team, whose ultimate goal would be to prove beyond a reasonable doubt that McVeigh and Nichols were guilty of bombing the Murrah building and should be sentenced to death for their crime.

The lead prosecutor chosen to try the government's case was Assistant U.S. Attorney Joseph Hartzler from Illinois. Hartzler had fourteen years of experience with both the criminal and civil divisions of the Department of Justice's Chicago office. He counted among his victories four convictions against a domestic terrorist group that attempted to blow up a Chicago building ten years earlier. Joining him would be Arlene Joplin, a federal prosecutor based in Oklahoma who had previously tried a number of death-penalty cases.

Joseph Hartzler was the chief prosecutor in the Oklahoma City bombing case.

Since McVeigh did not have the money to hire his own counsel, the government was legally required to provide him with an attorney. Public defender Susan Otto took up the task of defending McVeigh, and she chose John Coyle, a private defense attorney, to assist her. They stood by McVeigh's side when he was initially charged on April 21 and at another hearing on April 27 at El Reno federal prison in Oklahoma, and they also met with their client to discuss the defense strategy. Otto and Coyle were well respected in Oklahoma for their work, but after a few days of working with McVeigh they realized they could no longer represent him.

Both attorneys had often worked in the federal courthouse near the Murrah building, and they knew people who were injured or killed in the bombing. Otto's office had been damaged

Timothy McVeigh, center, meets with his lawyers Stephen Jones, right, and Robert Nigh.

in the bombing, and Coyle admitted receiving death threats. These facts constituted an emotional involvement with the bombing that Otto and Coyle believed would affect their ability to defend McVeigh.

On May 8, 1995, Otto and Coyle were replaced by Stephen Jones, who took the assignment at the request of David Russell, the chief judge of the Western District of Oklahoma. Jones had a solid career in both law and politics, and his résumé included work for Richard Nixon and for the American Civil Liberties Union. Defending McVeigh was a job that no attorney really wanted, but the American justice system demanded that he receive representation. The Sixth Amendment to the Constitution provides that those accused of crimes have the right to a speedy and public trial, and they also have the right to counsel for their defense. "Even a man accused of the worst act of terrorism ever committed in this country," Jones writes in his book *Others Unknown: Timothy McVeigh and the Oklahoma City Bombing Conspiracy*, "is entitled to the best defense possible. This concept is a cornerstone of our system of justice."[28]

Challenges for the Defense

Jones assembled his legal team and began the work of creating a defense for McVeigh. Another attorney, Michael Tigar, was appointed to defend Terry Nichols, but at this point the assumption was that both men would be tried together. With the defense team in place, Jones set about doing his own investigative work to build a defense around his now-notorious client. The government prosecutors had a much greater array of resources than those afforded Jones, and they had a three-week head start.

Another problem Jones ran into is that few people were willing to help him, since McVeigh's guilt had been presumed in many circles outside the judicial branch. He recounts experiencing a complete lack of cooperation from FBI agents and Justice Department employees. For instance, Jones's team was not allowed to closely examine the bomb crater at the crime scene. They also faced extended, unexplained delays when they requested FBI 302s and evidence reports for review.

Jones was also rebuffed by a number of witnesses he attempted to interview. "Hadn't they already told the FBI—and the media—all they knew?" Jones wrote. "Besides, wasn't McVeigh guilty as sin?"[29] This was a result not only of the head start that the FBI had in conducting their investigation, but the extensive media coverage which had already portrayed McVeigh as guilty.

These difficulties for the defense in preparing its case were the first of a number of contentious issues that had to be addressed. They would lead to a series of pretrial hearings and motions that would delay the trial for almost two years.

Changing the Judge and the Trial Venue

McVeigh and Nichols were formally indicted by a grand jury for the Oklahoma City bombing on August 10, 1995. They faced eleven counts, including the conspiracy to use, and using, a weapon of mass destruction, destroying federal property with explosives, and the murder of eight law enforcement officers who died in the explosion while on duty. This arraignment hearing signaled that the government was confident that it had enough evidence to convict the two men in a court of law. U.S. district court judge Wayne Alley was assigned to preside over the trial, which he set for May 17, 1996. His appointment, however, was controversial and raised alarm with both the defense and the prosecution.

Alley's office and courtroom were in the federal courthouse near the Murrah building and were severely damaged in the bombing. As with Otto and Coyle, his impartiality came into question, and Jones requested that he recuse, or remove, himself from the case. The prosecution agreed with this sentiment. They did not want their case against McVeigh and Nichols to be compromised if Alley's integrity came into question.

The U.S. District Court System in the Oklahoma City Bombing Trial

There are ninety-four U.S. district courts in the fifty states plus Puerto Rico, the Virgin Islands, the District of Columbia, Guam, and the Northern Mariana Islands. Oklahoma has three judicial districts—Northern, Eastern, and Western. The federal trial of Timothy McVeigh would ordinarily have taken place in the Western District in Oklahoma City. However, since the courthouse was damaged in the bombing and it was ruled that McVeigh could not receive a fair trial there, the trial was moved to Colorado, with one judicial district based in Denver.

The federal courts of appeal are organized into thirteen judicial circuits, each served by a court of appeals. Oklahoma and Colorado are in the Tenth Circuit, which is served by twelve judges. This is the circuit where McVeigh's appeals were heard and ultimately rejected.

Source: The U.S. Courts. www.uscourts.gov/faq.html.

Alley refused to step down, but he did make a motion to move the trial to Lawton, Oklahoma, 90 miles (145km) southwest of Oklahoma City, because he recognized the inability to recruit an impartial jury in the city where the bombing took place. His refusal prompted Jones to petition the U.S. Court of Appeals for the Tenth Circuit to request that Alley be removed from the case. On December 1, 1995, the court of appeals removed Alley and replaced him with chief district court judge Richard Matsch of Colorado.

Matsch had served on the federal bench since his appointment in 1974. He had a reputation as a tough but fair judge who had no tolerance for attorneys who entered his courtroom unprepared. He also had experience in dealing with extremist groups, having presided over the 1987 trial of the Silent Brotherhood, a neo-Nazi group that had committed robbery and murder in an effort to stir a racist revolution in America.

His first task as presiding judge was to review Jones's request for a change of venue out of Oklahoma to another state. When Alley had moved the trial out of Oklahoma City to Lawton, Oklahoma, he stated, "It is far enough to provide a trial setting appropriate for detached and dispassionate deliberation."[30] Jones, however, felt that all of Oklahoma should be off-limits for the trial because of the angry atmosphere that pervaded the entire state. He pointed to the fact that Governor Frank Keating had referred to McVeigh and Nichols as "creeps" and a number of editorial clippings from Oklahoma newspapers as evidence that an impartial jury could not be found anywhere in the state. Matsch ruled on February 20, 1996, that the trial was to be held in Denver, Colorado, and reset the trial date to March 31, 1997.

Separate Trials

Jones and Tigar also petitioned Matsch to sever the trial of McVeigh and Nichols so that the two men could be tried separately. Nichols's statements to the FBI after he turned himself in placed McVeigh at the head of the bombing conspiracy, and his defense would be based on the fact that McVeigh had in one way or another coerced him into taking part. As potential members of a conspiracy, it is common for two or more defendants to be tried together, and Hartzler felt that this case should be no different. Trying the two men together would allow for a speedy trial that was less of a burden on the taxpayers.

Jones maintained that his client would not be able to get a fair trial in these circumstances. In a brief Jones filed to the court on September 4, 1996, he wrote, "To the extent the Government's evidence reveals activity which can be taken as 'incriminating,' each defendant has a powerful incentive to attribute such activity to his codefendant."[31]

The Charges Against Timothy James McVeigh and Terry Lynn Nichols

Count One: Conspiracy to Use a Weapon of Mass Destruction, in violation of Title 18, U.S. Code, Section 2332a.

Count Two: Use of a Weapon of Mass Destruction, in violation of Title 18, U.S. Code, Sections 2332a and 2(a)&(b).

Count Three: Destruction by Explosive, in violation of Title 18, U.S. Code, Sections 844(f) and 2(a)&(b).

Count Four: *First Degree Murder, Mickey Bryant Maroney, special agent, U.S. Secret Service.

Count Five: *First Degree Murder, Donald R. Leonard, special agent, U.S. Secret Service.

Count Six: *First Degree Murder, Alan Gerald Whicher, assistant special agent in charge, U.S. Secret Service.

Count Seven: *First Degree Murder, Cynthia Lynn Campbell-Brown, special agent, U.S. Secret Service.

Count Eight: *First Degree Murder, Kenneth Glenn McCullough, special agent, U.S. Drug Enforcement Administration.

Count Nine: *First Degree Murder, Paul Douglas Ice, special agent, U.S. Customs Service.

Count Ten: *First Degree Murder, Claude Arthur Medearis, special agent, U.S. Customs Service.

Count Eleven: *First Degree Murder, Paul G. Broxterman, special agent, Department of Housing and Urban Development.

*In violation of Title 18, U.S. Code, Sections 1114, 1111 and 2(a)&(b); and Title 28, Code of Federal Regulations, Section 64.2(h).

71

On October 25, 1996, Matsch ruled that McVeigh and Nichols would be tried separately, with the Nichols trial to take place after McVeigh's.

The FBI Crime Lab Comes Under Scrutiny

The FBI crime laboratory had long been considered one of the best crime labs in the country. Evidence that had been shipped there and analyzed by trained forensic science experts had brought successful convictions in numerous cases. However, an eighteen-month investigation by the Office of the Inspector General (OIG) in the Department of Justice discovered a number of improper examination procedures, faulty reports, and poor management oversight in several key federal cases, among them the Oklahoma City bombing.

The FBI crime lab compromises five areas: the Scientific Analysis Section (SAS), the Latent Fingerprint Section, the Special Projects Section, the Forensic Science Research and Training Center (FSRTC), and the Investigative Operations and Support Section. The Scientific Analysis Section is responsible for all forensic examinations and is subdivided into a number of units based on category. The three areas that the report focused on were the Explosives Unit, the Materials Analysis Unit, and the Chemistry-Toxicology Unit.

The report became public in April 1997 just days before the McVeigh trial was set to begin. It determined that Explosives Unit examiner David Williams had reached his conclusions about the size and makeup of the bomb in an unscientific manner. In determining that the main charge was ANFO, the OIG report stated, "Williams did not draw a valid scientific conclusion but rather speculated from the fact that one of the defendants purchased ANFO components. His estimate of the weight of the main charge was too specific, and again was based in part on the improper, non-scientific ground of what a defendant had allegedly purchased."[32]

Items that were to be examined and used as evidence were also handled improperly. The clothes that McVeigh was wearing when he was arrested were shipped to the crime lab in a brown paper bag rather than in a sealed evidence bag as procedure requires. In fact, there were several pieces of bomb debris that had to be discarded because they were exposed to other items from the bomb site and mixed with other chemical residues, thereby mixing the particles and confusing the findings.

The potential for evidence that directly linked McVeigh and Nichols to the bombing being thrown out had federal prosecutors quite worried. Jones wanted to exploit the issue of faulty forensic evidence to plant doubt in the mind of the jury. He petitioned the court to have the OIG report presented at the trial, but Matsch ruled that the full report, which also examined lab procedures in other cases, was not relevant. He allowed only 6 of the 517 pages to be entered into evidence. In essence, Jones could make note of the circumstantial aspect of the crime lab's findings, but those findings would not be rejected in the trial or in the minds of the jury.

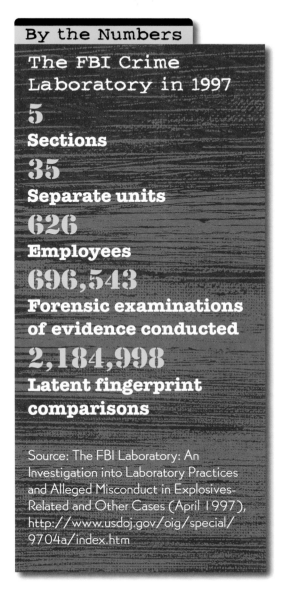

By the Numbers

The FBI Crime Laboratory in 1997

5
Sections

35
Separate units

626
Employees

696,543
Forensic examinations of evidence conducted

2,184,998
Latent fingerprint comparisons

Source: The FBI Laboratory: An Investigation into Laboratory Practices and Alleged Misconduct in Explosives-Related and Other Cases (April 1997), http://www.usdoj.gov/oig/special/9704a/index.htm

Jury Selection in the McVeigh Trial

In the American judicial system the guilt or innocence of the accused is decided by a jury of their peers. Jurors are selected at random from the community in which a trial is scheduled

U.S. attorneys Patrick Ryan, left, Aitan Goelman, and Beth Wilkinson leave the courthouse in Denver after presenting the prosecution's case in the McVeigh trial.

to take place, and they are screened by the prosecution and the defense to prevent people with any conceivable biases against the defendant's race, color, ethnicity, religious affiliation, or background from deciding the defendant's fate. Defenders and prosecutors also seek to prevent anyone with any reasonable knowledge of the case from sitting on a jury, because that person's knowledge could also predispose them, consciously or unconsciously, to make a certain judgment in a case before they have heard the evidence.

It was nearly impossible to find potential jurors, even in Denver, that did not have at least some knowledge of the Oklahoma City bombing and the story of Timothy McVeigh. For the preceding two years, magazine articles, newspaper editorials, television shows, and books focused on the tragedy of Oklahoma City. Virtually every conspiracy theory imaginable was entertained as to who actually committed the bombing, and just what role, if any, McVeigh played in it. With these facts in mind, jury selection was expected to be rigorous.

Ninety-nine Colorado residents reported for jury selection on March 31, 1997, and each of them was thoroughly questioned by the prosecution and the defense. Some were dismissed because of their opposition to the death penalty. One man was dismissed because he knew someone who was killed in the bombing. Still others were dismissed because they were tax protestors or held vehement opinions for or against the Second Amendment.

After three weeks, twelve jurors and six alternates were chosen to listen to the case against Timothy McVeigh and decide his fate. There were blue-collar workers, military service veterans, retirees, and teachers among them. They were seated on April 22, 1997, and sequestered so that their identities would not be known to the public.

In such high-profile cases as this one, it is a common practice for judges to sequester a jury in an undisclosed location. This is done to prevent them from being contacted by the media, with which they are not allowed to communicate, or by anyone who may wish to unduly influence their verdict through threats, coercion, or bribery.

The jury, the courthouse, and the temporary residences of the prosecution and defense teams were provided heavy security during the trial, which was scheduled to begin on April 24, 1997, two years and five days after the bombing in Oklahoma City. Though the prosecution would attempt to prove that there was no one else involved in the bombing beyond McVeigh and Nichols, law enforcement officers were not going to leave anything to chance. They were worried that someone might try to assassinate McVeigh or attack the courthouse in a show of extremist support. With the realization that such a horrifying attack as the one that destroyed the Murrah federal building could be perpetrated by American extremists, many felt that anything was possible.

Justice Sought and Justice Found

The opening proceedings in the case of *The United States v. Timothy J. McVeigh* were a highly anticipated event. The families of the bombing victims and the survivors gathered in an auditorium in Oklahoma City to view the trial on closed circuit television, anxious for justice. Reporters huddled outside the federal courthouse in Denver, engaging in speculation and relaying any information they could find to curious citizens around the country. Inside the courtroom both the prosecution and the defense prepared to present their case, each confident that the extensive work completed to this point would yield a favorable outcome.

For the prosecution's part, Hartzler wanted to prove to the jury that McVeigh committed the bombing that killed 168 people. He would not elaborate on the theories of a wider conspiracy or even entertain the thought that other perpetrators aside from Terry Nichols were involved. He did not intend to spend much time on the forensic evidence, some of which was still considered circumstantial and questionable after the report on faulty FBI lab procedures became public. Instead, Hartzler focused on what was specifically known, and he traced McVeigh's steps in the months leading up to the bombing.

Hartzler also gave many victims of the bombing an opportunity to take the stand and describe the horrors of April 19, 1995, a move that was controversial and, in Jones's view, objectionable in a court of law. "Justice . . . is blind to sympathy, blind to compassion, blind to agony," Jones writes in *Others Unknown*. "Justice is blind to these considerations so that they do not influence or prejudice the search for the right verdict under law."[33] In Jones's view, the jury would undoubtedly be influenced by the numerous stories told by parents who lost their children and husbands and wives who lost their spouses. Emotion could cloud their judgment, even if they maintained that it would not.

For the defense's part, Jones wanted to take the attention away from the bombing itself and concentrate on the conduct of the government's investigation of the case. He focused on unanswered questions that were circulating about McVeigh's role in the attack. Did he act alone or was he part of a conspiracy? If he was at all involved, was he the ringleader as the prosecution suggested, or just a trigger man for some as yet unidentified criminal mastermind? Jones did not so much want to prove McVeigh's innocence as he wanted to make the jury doubt that he was solely responsible. This was the only strategy Jones believed could keep his client from being sentenced to death.

The Body of Evidence

In criminal trials, both the prosecution and the defense are allowed to make opening statements, which lay out their cases for and against, respectively, the guilt of the defendant. Hartzler's opening statement emphasized the rage that drove McVeigh to bomb the Murrah building and the emotional toll it had on the victims. Jones emphasized the inconsistencies that existed in the government's forensic evidence. "If Tim McVeigh built the bomb and put it in the truck," he told the jury, "our proof will be that his fingernails, his nostrils, his hair . . . would have it all over them. They don't. Out of 7,000 pounds of debris, there are fewer than half a dozen pieces of evidence of a forensic nature."[34] He also advanced the theory that McVeigh was not the man they were looking for but that there were others involved.

The prosecution took eighteen days to present its case and called 137 witnesses. They noted that six storage lockers had been rented by McVeigh and Nichols during the fall of 1994, some of them under aliases. Jones maintained that not all these

Becoming a U.S. Attorney

Job Description:
Working as an attorney for the U.S. Department of Justice can be a time-intensive but rewarding occupation. Attorneys represent the U.S. government in a variety of areas, including antitrust cases, bankruptcy, civil rights, criminal cases, and immigration. U.S. attorneys generally work for the attorney general, the Bureau of Alcohol, Tobacco, Firearms and Explosives, the Federal Bureau of Investigation, the Bureau of Prisons, the Tax Division, the U.S. Marshals Service, and the Drug Enforcement Administration, among others.

Education:
Four years of college, plus a Juris Doctor (J.D., or law degree), which generally takes three years of law school to achieve.

Qualifications:
Each department has its own list of qualifications, but an experienced attorney must be an active member of a bar association in any jurisdiction, plus have one to three years of post-J.D. experience. There are openings for entry-level attorneys with solid academic, moot court, and work and extracurricular experience related to the position. All candidates must have excellent oral and written communication skills, strong character, and analytical skills.

Additional Information:
Travel is often required in this work, and the hours can be long.

Salary:
$40,000 to $140,000 per year, based on experience, plus locality pay, which is a pay adjustment based on the cost of living, which can differ in certain areas of the country.

Source: U.S. Department of Justice Office of Attorney Recruitment and Management. www.usdoj.gov/oarm.

aliases were incriminating, pointing to the fact that Nichols often hid his household belongings in various storage lockers to prevent creditors from repossessing them. Even if that were true, it did not help McVeigh's case or explain the vast amounts of explosive materials that were stored in the lockers.

By presenting that list of materials to the jury, the prosecution had proven that McVeigh and Nichols had in their possession the components necessary to construct a bomb large enough to destroy the Murrah building. However, as discussed earlier, the methods used to determine the chemical makeup of the bomb had come into question due to faulty procedures at the FBI crime lab. Jones attempted to exploit this hole in the prosecution's case by pointing out that "experts could not determine whether the main charge—the ANFO itself—was exploded through a three- or four-step explosive train, or by using an electric or non-electric blasting cap."[35]

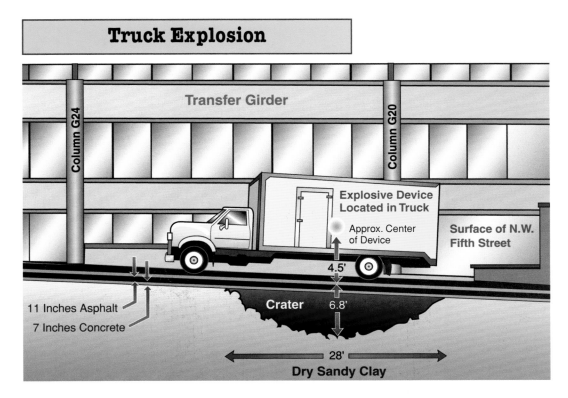

Truck Explosion

Transfer Girder

Column G24

Column G20

Explosive Device
Located in Truck

Approx. Center
of Device

Surface of N.W.
Fifth Street

4.5'

11 Inches Asphalt

7 Inches Concrete

Crater   6.8'

28'

Dry Sandy Clay

Since the elements that made up the bomb were incinerated in the explosion, forensics experts could only theorize as to whether the ANFO was ignited by the blasting caps stolen from the Martin Marietta quarry or by an explosive train, which is a series of smaller charges set off in rapid succession in a delayed explosion.

The circumstantial evidence surrounding the exact makeup of the bomb had little effect on the jury. It mattered little to them how the bomb was detonated. What did have an impact were the witnesses that the prosecution presented and the manner in which it proceeded with its case. "Witnesses and evidence have been presented so rapidly and questioned so narrowly," reported the *New York Times,* "that lawyers for Mr. McVeigh have found few openings to widen the scope of questions."[36]

Several of the witnesses testified to seeing McVeigh and Nichols at several key points—renting the Ryder truck and purchasing large amounts of ammonium nitrate and fuel oil. One witness testified seeing a large Ryder truck at Geary State Fishing Lake in Kansas two days before the bombing. It was there that McVeigh was believed to have actually built the bomb. Other witnesses testified to their experiences as survivors of the bombing, or they discussed the loss of family members and how they tried to rebuild their lives. These testimonies did not further prove McVeigh's involvement in the attack, but it did appeal to the jurors' emotional sensibilities.

The Prosecution's Star Witnesses

There were three more witnesses that, more than any others, helped seal the prosecution's case, and their testimonies were a significant blow to the defense. Michael and Lori Fortier and McVeigh's sister Jennifer all had intimate knowledge of either the plan for the bombing or the factors that motivated McVeigh to commit the crime. All of them had spent time in the custody of the FBI, and all were looking at time in prison because they had prior knowledge of the attack but failed to warn the authorities.

McVeigh had spent a lot of time with the Fortiers at their home in Arizona during the two years between the Waco tragedy and the Oklahoma City bombing. Both Michael and Lori testified that McVeigh had been extremely angry about Waco and that he planned to exact revenge against the government. Michael testified that McVeigh told him he had learned how to convert a truck into a bomb and that he planned

The Mysterious Extra Leg

One popular conspiracy theory revolves around the fact that McVeigh was not alone when he drove the Ryder truck up to the Murrah building on April 19, 1995. Some witnesses maintained they saw another person with him, and there are those who believe that this person may have perished in the blast. In an attempt to lend credence to this idea, conspiracy theorists point to an unidentified leg that was found at the bomb site.

This leg was dressed in an olive-drab pant leg with a black military boot, and, at first examination, appeared to belong to a dark-haired man less than thirty years of age. In a conclusive leap, conspiracy theorists maintain that this must be the body part of a bomber since the bombers were in military dress. No account is taken for the military personnel that often came and went from the government offices that existed in the Murrah building.

In February 1996 medical examiners identified the leg and determined that it belonged to Lakesha Levy, a twenty-one-year-old black woman who was an airman first class in the air force. Her body had been found on April 27, and she was apparently buried with the wrong leg. The major discrepancy in identifying the race and gender of the person to whom the leg belonged was discovered when further FBI analysis yielded more conclusive results than the preliminary examination by the Oklahoma state medical examiner.

to use it against a federal building. He had even built a small version of the device in a sports bottle and invited Michael to witness a test detonation, but Michael refused. Michael also revealed to the jury how McVeigh had picked his target, stating that McVeigh believed that the orders to attack the Branch Davidian compound in Waco had originated in the ATF offices in Oklahoma City.

In reality, McVeigh had considered several criteria in choosing his target among a number of federal office buildings in Arkansas, Texas, and other states. In extensive interviews he gave to Michel and Herbeck in preparation for their book *American Terrorist,* McVeigh stated that he wanted to strike a building that housed offices for the ATF, FBI, and the DEA. The building also had to be home to a large number of federal workers because they were guilty of conspiring in the government's tyranny over the people.

After scouting different locations, McVeigh chose the Murrah building because its large glass facade made it vulnerable to an explosion. It was also located opposite a large parking lot that would allow the blast to dissipate in the open air, minimizing collateral damage. McVeigh admitted wanting to kill as many federal employees as possible, but he claimed that he did not want to injure any nongovernment employees if he could help it. He wanted to confine the casualties only to those who served the government.

McVeigh also told Michel and Herbeck that Michael Fortier actually joined him in his scouting mission to Oklahoma City, but this point was never brought up when Fortier testified at McVeigh's trial. Fortier did tell the jury that he wanted no part of McVeigh's plan, but he was not completely removed from it, either. McVeigh told Fortier about his plans in detail, and Fortier had helped McVeigh traffic firearms that he claimed were stolen from a gun dealer in Arkansas to help pay for the bomb plot. Some of the guns from this robbery were found in Terry Nichols's home in Herington, Kansas.

Fortier was challenged by the defense on cross-examination. Jones reminded the jury that Fortier had intimate details of the bombing from the time that the plot was hatched, yet he did not alert the authorities. He also held antigovernment beliefs not much different from McVeigh or Nichols, he was an abuser of illegal drugs, and in the days after the bombing he had maintained that McVeigh was innocent. He still had a motive to lie to the jury; his testimony had earned him a plea deal in which the government would sentence him to twelve years and not seek the death penalty against him.

By the Numbers

Financial Cost of the Oklahoma City Bombing

$15 MILLION
Cost of defense of Timothy McVeigh, paid by government [3]

$5,000
Approximate cost of materials used to make the truck bomb, excluding the estimated value of the truck itself. [4]

3. Source: Oklahoma City Bombing timeline, *Indianapolis Star* Library Fact Files, IndyStar.com, http://www2.indystar.com/library/factfiles/crime/national/1995/oklahoma_city_bombing/ok.html

4. Source: Lou Michel and Dan Herbeck, *American Terrorist: Timothy McVeigh and the Oklahoma City Bombing*. New York, Regan , 2001, p. 176.

Fortier's character had been called into question, but his wife Lori corroborated his testimony with a chilling detail that stuck in the minds of the jury. In the fall of 1994 McVeigh spent time in the Fortiers' home working on a design for the truck bomb. Lori recalled to the jury that McVeigh demonstrated to her what the bomb would look like by lining up soup cans on their kitchen floor.

Jennifer McVeigh also provided the jury with information about her brother that established the mind-set that drew him to bomb the Murrah building. When she had been questioned in 1995 following the bombing, she refused to cooperate with the FBI. They had found numerous letters, written to her by her brother over the previous two years, detailing his antigovernment philosophy and his anger over Waco. He had encouraged her to read *The Turner Diaries* and other similar literature. He also spun stories about being on secret missions and encouraged Jennifer to burn his letters after she read them. In one letter which she did burn, he alluded to his plans when he told her that "something big" was going to happen in the month of April 1995.

Several of the letters did survive, and Jennifer was questioned about them at the trial. Tim had sent her a number of his belongings in the months leading up to the bombing and had concluded one of his last letters with the words, "won't be back forever." These actions had disturbed Jennifer, but, at Tim's insistence, she did not share the letters with anyone. She looked up to her brother, and she feared that he had become involved in something very dangerous, but she did not realize how dangerous until she learned from the television news that he was in custody for the Oklahoma City bombing.

Jennifer McVeigh's testimony, along with that of Michael and Lori Fortier, had a devastating impact on McVeigh's defense. With their words, the prosecution was able to fulfill its task of convincing the jury that Timothy McVeigh was an angry man capable of committing a crime as horrible as killing 168 people. The defense hoped to produce as powerful a witness to at least refute the prosecution's theory that McVeigh acted alone.

McVeigh's Conviction and Appeal

In order to lessen the sentence that McVeigh faced if convicted, Jones had hoped to illustrate that a broader conspiracy had been responsible for the bombing. Unfortunately, the principal witness that the defense hoped would at least poke a hole in the theory that McVeigh acted alone, or only with Nichols, did not perform as expected. Bradley, the survivor of the bombing who had to have her leg amputated before she could be removed from the wreckage, told authorities in 1995 that she remembered a dark-complexioned man leaving the passenger side of the Ryder truck after it was parked in front of the Murrah building moments before the explosion. However, once she was on the stand under cross-examination, she admitted that she did not actually get a good look at the man and that he could have been McVeigh. It was also revealed during cross-examination that Bradley had memory problems and had spent time in mental institutions during her childhood. This destroyed her credibility as a witness and significantly impaired Jones's conspiracy theory.

Daina Bradley, a survivor of the bombing, testified at McVeigh's trial.

The entire defense portion of the case lasted only three and a half days, with twenty-five witnesses being called upon. After the closing statements were made by both sides, the jury began their deliberations. During this time the jury discussed the case in detail in closed quarters, going over the testimony of the witnesses and the evidence presented to them. On

June 2, 1997, they concluded that McVeigh was guilty on all eleven counts he was charged with. On June 13 the jury further decided that McVeigh be put to death, and on August 14 Matsch formally sentenced McVeigh to die by lethal injection.

McVeigh took the opportunity Matsch gave him to make a statement at his sentencing hearing by quoting Supreme Court justice Louis Brandeis, a fierce proponent of individual rights. The quote is from Brandeis's dissenting opinion, or an opinion that disagrees with the Court's majority verdict, in a 1928 case that affirmed the right of prosecutors to use phone wiretaps in criminal cases. "Our government is the potent, the omnipresent teacher. For good or ill, it teaches the whole people by its example."[37]

According to law, McVeigh was entitled to appeal the verdict before the federal court of appeals, but he fired Jones as his attorney before going forward. McVeigh felt that Jones did not represent him in a manner that allowed his real reasons for

Timothy McVeigh's lawyers: Chris Tritico, left, Robert Nigh, center, and Richard Burr.

committing the bombing to become known. He resented his defense team's spending time chasing down far-flung leads trying to prove there was a larger conspiracy, despite the fact that Jones did so in an attempt to spare McVeigh's life. Rob Nigh, who also worked on McVeigh's defense, took over during the appeals process.

Nigh wrote to the U.S. Court of Appeals for the Tenth Circuit that McVeigh's case should be reconsidered because the emotional impact of the survivors and family members of the victims prejudiced the jury against McVeigh. On September 8, 1998, the appeals court ruled that McVeigh was fairly convicted and sentenced. On March 9, 1999, a further appeal to the U.S. Supreme Court resulted in a refusal to hear his case. On July 13 McVeigh was transported to a federal penitentiary in Terre Haute, Indiana, where he awaited execution.

The Trial of Terry Nichols

While McVeigh moved unsuccessfully through the appeals process, Terry Nichols went on trial. A fresh prosecution team was brought in, but Tigar, Nichols's attorney, had been present during the McVeigh trial and was well versed in the evidence that would be brought against his client. Tigar was motivated to keep Nichols from being sentenced to death as McVeigh had been, and in order to do so he needed to minimize the role Nichols was believed to have played in planning and executing the bombing. Unfortunately for the defense, two robberies committed for the larger purpose of putting together the bomb plot were undeniably linked to Nichols in the trial, which began on November 3, 1997.

The prosecution revisited the details of the robbery at the Martin Marietta quarry and tried to tie the robbery to Nichols because tool marks from the drilled padlocks matched those of a drill bit found in Nichols's home in Kansas. Tigar was successful in deflecting this charge, noting that thousands of drill bits could have created the same marks. Matsch instructed the jury to disregard this piece of evidence. However, Nichols could not duck the charge that he was involved in the robbery of an Arkansas gun dealer which yielded thousands of dollars in cash, guns, and precious metals and gems. Several of the guns reported stolen from the robbery were found during the preliminary search of Nichols's home and storage lockers in 1995, as well as the key to a safe deposit box that belonged to the dealer.

The testimony of FBI agent Stephen Smith was also damaging to Nichols. He testified that during the seven-hour interview with Nichols on April 21, 1995, Nichols admitted to driving to Oklahoma City on April 16, Easter Sunday, to pick up McVeigh. Nichols claimed that McVeigh's car had broken down in Oklahoma City and that McVeigh wanted Nichols to give him a ride back to Junction City. In reality, McVeigh had stashed his getaway car, the 1977 Mercury, and needed someone to bring him back to Junction City to rent the Ryder truck.

It was actually Michael Fortier's testimony at the Nichols trial that may have saved him from the death penalty. While Fortier's appearance at McVeigh's trial helped condemn McVeigh to death, Fortier testified, "Tim told me that Terry

During Terry Nichols's 2003 hearing, witness Ruth Kailey testified that she saw a yellow Ryder truck behind Nichols's residence before the 1995 bombing.

Michael Fortier testifies at the trial of Terry Nichols in April 2004.

no longer wanted to help him mix the bomb."[38] Tigar attacked Fortier's character and motivation for testifying, as did Jones during the McVeigh trial, and Fortier told him that Nichols had never spoken to him about bombing a building.

Terry Nichols was found guilty of conspiracy charges and involuntary manslaughter, but he was acquitted of murder on December 23, 1997. Matsch offered Nichols leniency in sentencing if he cooperated with the government in learning more about the conspiracy. Nichols refused and, on June 4, 1998, was sentenced to life in prison without the possibility of parole.

Nichols's refusal to elaborate on the plot to blow up the Murrah building effectively ended the federal government's prosecution of the Oklahoma City bombing. McVeigh gave up his right to further appeals and his execution date was set for May 16, 2001. Fortier was sentenced to twelve years in prison for failing to notify authorities of the bomb plot.

The families of the victims of the Oklahoma City bombing settled with the outcome, believing justice had been served, and went about trying to rebuild their lives. However, the legal drama was not over, and there were many issues still to be addressed.

Open Wounds and Unanswered Questions

A Shocking Turn of Events

On May 10, 2001, just six days before McVeigh was scheduled to be executed by lethal injection for the Oklahoma City bombing, the Justice Department announced that 3,135 pages of FBI interviews, photographs, and other evidence had not been made available to the defense during the discovery, or preparation, phase of the trial. "While the Department is confident the documents do not in any way create any reasonable doubt about McVeigh's guilt," Justice Department spokesperson Mindy Tucker said, "the Department is concerned that McVeigh's attorneys were not able to review them at the appropriate time."[39]

The discovery of the missing documents spurred conspiracy theories that the government had deliberately manipulated evidence in McVeigh's trial. His execution was postponed for one month while his attorneys reviewed the documents. The misplacement of the documents was due to a filing error in the FBI system, and Attorney General John Ashcroft defended the government's actions. "The new documents represent only a small fraction of one percent of the total number of produced documents in this case," Ashcroft wrote in a press release. "This item-by-item review has revealed that none, *none* of these new documents raised any doubt about the proven and admitted guilt of Timothy McVeigh."[40]

McVeigh's attorneys attempted to postpone his execution on June 7, but Matsch rejected the plea, stating that nothing in the documents proved McVeigh's innocence or invalidated the jury's death sentence.

McVeigh was executed by lethal injection on June 11, 2001, before a small group of witnesses at the federal prison in Terre Haute, Indiana. Other witnesses viewed the proceedings via closed-circuit television in Oklahoma City. In this process McVeigh was injected with sodium pentathol, which rendered him unconscious. He was then injected with pancuronium bromide, which paralyzed all his voluntary muscles. Finally, he was injected with a solution of potassium chloride, which in high concentrations causes cardiac arrest.

Prosecutors representing the state of Oklahoma indicted Terry Nichols on state murder charges in an attempt to get him sentenced to death for his role in the bombing. Nichols was

---

KOHN, KOHN & COLAPINTO, P.C.
ATTORNEYS AT LAW
3233 P STREET, N.W.
WASHINGTON, DC 20007-2756

TELEPHONE (202) 342-6980   TELECOPIER (202) 342-6984

June 1, 2001

Via Facsimile and By Hand
Fax Number: (202) 307-6777

URGENT MATTER
FOR THE IMMEDIATE ATTENTION
OF THE ATTORNEY GENERAL

Hon. John Ashcroft
Attorney General
U.S. Department of Justice
10th and Constitution Ave., N.W.
Washington, D.C. 20530

Re: OKBOMB ISSUES

Dear Attorney General Ashcroft:

We represent a number of former FBI employees who worked at the FBI crime lab. In the course of our investigation in a case related to this representation, we have documented serious concerns related to the prosecution of the Oklahoma City Bombing case ("OKBOMB") that call into question the integrity of evidence presented by the government during the OKBOMB prosecution. We believe that these concerns are most serious and that we are under an obligation to turn this information over to you so that you may fulfill your obligation to notify the defendants in the OKBOMB cases about these serious matters and take corrective action.

One of the government's witnesses in the OKBOMB case was Mr. Stephen Burmeister, a unit chief within the FBI crime lab. References to his testimony during the OKBOMB trial, *U.S. v. McVeigh*, used in this letter shall be identified as "McVeigh Tr. –." Mr. Burmeister was also responsible for firing Dr. Jorge Villanueva, a Ph.D. chemist who was employed in the FBI crime lab in 1996 and 1997. That wrongful discharge case is currently pending in U.S. District Court on both a First Amendment reprisal theory and pursuant to Title VII of the Civil Rights Act of 1964. *See, Villanueva, et al. v. FBI, et al.*, C.A. No. 1:98CV1704 (D.D.C.). On May 15, 2001, Mr. Burmeister gave sworn deposition testimony in the *Villanueva* case. References to his deposition testimony shall be identified as "Deposition Tr. –." Also, the relevant pages from Mr. Burmeister's deposition are being included as attachments to this letter.

The letter to Attorney General John Ashcroft, which states there were "serious concerns" about misconduct inside the FBI crime lab during the Oklahoma City bombing investigation.

The Oklahoma City National Memorial, which was dedicated on April 19, 2000.

tried and found guilty of 161 counts of first-degree murder and was sentenced again to life in prison on August 9, 2005.

The Memorial

In Oklahoma City, on the spot where the Alfred P. Murrah building once stood, is a memorial that was dedicated on April 19, 2000. It consists of a reflecting pool and an array of 168 chairs—149 large chairs representing the adults who were murdered in the bombing, and 19 small chairs representing the children killed that day.

Every year on April 19, relatives, friends, and their supporters gather for a memorial service to honor those who lost their lives in the Oklahoma City bombing. They pray, they share time with each other and offer mutual support, and they remember the vibrant lives cut short by a terrible act committed by an angry, vengeful man.

The Conspiracy That Will Not Die

The late discovery of the FBI files are just one of several questions that still remain for many who question the validity of the government's case against Timothy McVeigh. Key motions made by the court during his trial, including allowing emotional testimony of bombing survivors and disallowing the wider issue of the FBI crime lab's faulty work, drove some to believe that McVeigh never had a chance for a fair trial. His attorney Stephen Jones maintains that there was a wider international conspiracy in which McVeigh played only a small role.

Other journalists and professional writers have raised doubts about the government's case as well, believing that the bombing plot was hatched by foreign terrorists and that it was international in scope. They have held onto the questions about the identity of John Doe Number 2, despite his identity being established as someone unconnected with the bombing. There have been repeated inquiries about the man who was supposedly in the Ryder truck with McVeigh, even though no proof of his existence was ever found.

One possible reason for this continued belief that there was a wider plot to destroy the Murrah building is the implausibility of such a horrible crime being committed on American soil by just two American men, one of them a decorated war veteran. Even in a time when we are constantly under the threat of another terrorist strike, there is an innocence in the American character that refuses to acknowledge that such evil could live among us. This innocence is not a detriment to our way of life, but it can be costly if we do not recognize that there are indeed people that seek to harm innocent lives and that we have to defend ourselves against those people.

Notes

Introduction: The Seeds of Hatred

1. David Lohr, "Randy Weaver: Siege at Ruby Ridge," Court TV Crime Library, 2005. www.crimelibrary.com/gangsters_outlaws/cops_others/randy_weaver/8.html.

2. Quoted in Lou Michel and Dan Herbeck, *American Terrorist: Timothy McVeigh and the Oklahoma City Bombing*. New York: Regan, 2001, p. 120.

3. Edward S.G. Dennis Jr., "Evaluation of the Handling of the Branch Davidian Stand-off in Waco, Texas, " redacted version, U.S. Department of Justice, October 8, 1993, p. 3.

Chapter One: Declaring War on America

4. Quoted in Council on Foreign Relations, "A Conversation with Charles Schumer," transcript, January 25, 2002. www.cfr.org/publication/4317/conversation_with_charles_schumer.html.

5. Mark S. Hamm, *Apocalypse in Oklahoma: Waco and Ruby Ridge Revenged*. Boston: Northeastern University Press, 1997, p. 42.

6. Hamm, *Apocalypse in Oklahoma*, p. 43.

7. Quoted in Angel Franco, "Terror in Oklahoma: The Witnesses," *New York Times*, April 23, 1995.

8. Quoted in Richard A. Serrano, *One of Ours: Timothy McVeigh and the Oklahoma City Bombing*. New York: W.W. Norton, 1998, p. 154.

9. Quoted in Franco, "Terror In Oklahoma: The Witnesses," *New York Times*, April 23, 1995.

10. Quoted in Jayna Davis, *The Third Terrorist: The Middle East Connection to the Oklahoma City Bombing*. Nashville: WND, 2004, p. 18.

11. Chemical and Biological Arms Control Institute, *Critical Information Flows in the Alfred P. Murrah Building Bombing: A Case Study*. Washington, DC: CBACI, 2002, p. 28.

12. Hamm, *Apocalypse in Oklahoma*, p. 64.

Chapter Two: The Suspects

13. Quoted in Michel and Herbeck, *American Terrorist: Timothy McVeigh and the Oklahoma City Bombing*, p. 249.

14. Quoted in Davis, *The Third Terrorist*, p. 25.

15. Quoted in Sam Howe Verhovek, "Terror in Oklahoma: The Chase," *New York Times*, April 21, 1995.

16. Hamm, *Apocalypse in Oklahoma*, p. 77.

17. Michel and Herbeck, *American Terrorist*, p. 252.

18. Hamm, *Apocalypse in Oklahoma*, p. 90.

19. Sarah Rimer, "The Second Suspect," *New York Times*, May 28, 1995.

Chapter Three: On the Trail of Mass Murderers

20. Quoted in Serrano, *One of Ours*, p. 24.

21. Quoted in Hamm, *Apocalypse in Oklahoma*, p. 128.

22. Quoted in Hamm, *Apocalypse in Oklahoma*, p. 143.

23. Quoted in Serrano, *One of Ours*, p. 37.

24. Quoted in Serrano, *One of Ours*, p. 49.

25. Quoted in James Barron, "Terror in Oklahoma: The Suspect," *New York Times*, April 27, 1995.

26. Quoted in John Kifner, "The Gun Network: McVeigh's World," *New York Times*, July 5, 1995.

27. Michel and Herbeck, *American Terrorist*, p. 161.

Chapter Four: Pretrial Battles

28. Stephen Jones, *Others Unknown: Timothy McVeigh and the Oklahoma City Bombing Conspiracy*. New York: PublicAffairs, 2001, p. xxi.

29. Jones, *Others Unknown*, p. 36.

30. Quoted in CNN, "Oklahoma Bombing Judge Refuses to Step Down," September, 14, 1995. www.cnn.com/US/OKC/daily/9-14/index.html.

31. Stephen Jones et al., "Defendant McVeigh's Motion for Severance of Defendants and Brief in Support," *United States of America vs. Timothy James McVeigh and Terry Lynn Nichols*, Criminal Action No. 96-CR-68-M, September 4, 1996, Section I, paragraph 5.

32. Office of the Inspector General, U.S. Department of Justice, "The FBI Laboratory: An Investigation into Laboratory Practices and Alleged Misconduct in Explosives-Related and Other Cases," executive summary, April 1997, p. 8.

Chapter Five: Justice Sought and Justice Found

33. Jones, *Others Unknown*, p. 323.

34. Jones, *Others Unknown*, p. 322.

35. Jones, *Others Unknown*, p. 100.

36. Jo Thomas, "Swift, Hard Attack in Bombing Trial," *New York Times*, May 12, 1997.

37. Quoted in Michel and Herbeck, *American Terrorist*, p. 351.

38. Quoted in Jo Thomas, "Jury Hears of McVeigh Remarks About Nichols and Bomb Making," *New York Times*, November 14, 1997.

Epilogue: Open Wounds and Unanswered Questions

39. Quoted in David Johnston and Christopher Marquis, "U.S. Admits Failure to Share Evidence in McVeigh's Trial," *New York Times*, May 11, 2001.

40. John Ashcroft, "Attorney General Statement Regarding Timothy McVeigh," Office of the Attorney General, United States Department of Justice, May 24, 2001.

For More Information

Books

Jayna Davis, *The Third Terrorist: The Middle East Connection to the Oklahoma City Bombing.* Nashville: WND, 2004. Written by an investigative reporter working in Oklahoma City during the bombing, this book explores the theories behind foreign involvement in the attack.

Louis Freeh, *My FBI: Bringing Down the Mafia, Investigating Bill Clinton, and Fighting the War on Terror.* New York: St. Martin's, 2005. Autobiography of the man who was director of the FBI during the Oklahoma City bombing.

Mark S. Hamm, *Apocalypse in Oklahoma: Waco and Ruby Ridge Revenged.* Boston: Northeastern University Press, 1997. Explores how the ideology of the radical right motivated Timothy McVeigh and Terry Nichols to bomb the Murrah building.

Stuart H. James and Jon J. Nordby, eds., *Forensic Science: An Introduction to Scientific and Investigative Techniques,* 2nd ed. Boca Raton: CRC, 2005. Encyclopedic manual covering numerous aspects of forensic science and how crime scene investigations are performed.

Stephen Jones, *Others Unknown: Timothy McVeigh and the Oklahoma City Bombing Conspiracy.* New York: PublicAffairs, 2001. This updated edition details Jones's account of his work as McVeigh's defense attorney during his trial and includes his belief that there was a wider conspiracy behind the bombing.

Lou Michel and Dan Herbeck, *American Terrorist: Timothy McVeigh and the Oklahoma City Bombing.* New York: Regan, 2001. In-depth study of Timothy McVeigh by two journalists from the Buffalo area where McVeigh grew up. Includes exclusive interviews with McVeigh from prison.

Richard A. Serrano, *One of Ours: Timothy McVeigh and the Oklahoma City Bombing.* New York: W.W. Norton, 1998. A biography of Timothy McVeigh as well as a detailed account of the bombing itself with scores of interviews.

James Stinchcomb, *Opportunities in Law Enforcement and Criminal Justice Careers.* New York: McGraw-Hill, 2003. Lists a number of careers in law enforcement, giving information on qualifications, salaries, and the skills necessary to get jobs.

Reports

Chemical and Biological Arms Control Institute, *Critical Information Flows in the Alfred P. Murrah Building Bombing: A Case*

Study, 2002. The CBACI, established in 1994, is a policy research organization focusing on national and international security issues. This report studies the effectiveness of the response to the bombing and what was learned from the event.

Edward S.G. Dennis Jr., "Evaluation of the Handling of the Branch Davidian Standoff in Waco, Texas." Redacted version. U.S. Department of Justice, October 8, 1993. Explores the federal government's actions during the Waco siege, including negotiation tactics and the failure to bring a peaceful end to the situation.

Web Sites

Crime Library (www.crimelibrary.com). This site from Court TV offers detailed background and articles on the Oklahoma City bombing case, as well as the cases of Randy Weaver and the siege at Ruby Ridge and David Koresh and the Branch Davidian standoff.

The Federal Bureau of Investigation (www.fbi.gov). The FBI site is a great resource to learn about the bureau, the work that it does, and all the various departments that make up the nation's federal criminal investigative agency.

Oklahoma City National Memorial (www.oklahomacitynationalmemorial.org). A resource site for the Oklahoma City National Memorial & Museum built to honor and remember the victims of the Oklahoma City bombing.

The United States Department of Justice (www.usdoj.gov). Web site for the nation's law enforcement agency.

Index

Picture Credits

About the Author

This is Richard Brownell's third title for Lucent Books. His other books include *The Fall of the Confederacy and the End of Slavery* and *America's Failure in Vietnam,* which are part of Lucent's History's Great Defeats series. He has written two stage plays that have received numerous productions around the country, and he also writes political commentary for various periodicals and Internet sites. He holds a Bachelor of Fine Arts degree from New York University, where he was also recognized for Senior Achievement in Screenwriting. Brownell lives in New York City.